RETURN TO TRADITION

The
Revitalization
of
Turkish
Village
Carpets

JUNE ANDERSON

The California Academy of Sciences, San Francisco, California
in association with the University of Washington Press, Seattle and London

Photographs, unless specifically credited to others, and line drawings by the author

Turkish editing by Erhan Sarialp

English editing by Frances Bowles

Book design by Vivian Young

Printed and bound in Hong Kong

ISBN 0-295-97689-6

First published in the United States of America
by the University of Washington Press
P.O. Box 50096
Seattle, WA 98145-5096

Front cover: Carpet weaving in Yukariköy village, 1984. (Photo Harald Böhmer)

ACKNOWLEDGMENTS

Although it is the author who puts pen to paper, writing a book is usually a team effort, with many others contributing to the project. I am indebted to staff members of the Faculty of Fine Arts at Marmara University in Istanbul, including Dr. Harald Böhmer, Dr. Şerife Atlihan, Dr. Nevin Evez, and Dr. Erol Eti, for facilitating my visits to the carpet-weaving villages of western Turkey. Special thanks to Linda Robinson for escorting me to village homes and acting as interpreter. I am grateful to Lucia Amelia Martins and Bill McDonnell of Return to Tradition, the DOBAG carpet gallery in San Francisco, for making their inventory of Turkish carpets available for study purposes. For invaluable comments on the manuscript, my appreciation extends to Renate Böhmer, Robert Godbe, Dr. Archie Green, Dr. William Eschmeyer, Dr. Murray Eiland Jr., Keith Howell, and Dr. Nina Jablonski. Friends of Ethnic Art in San Francisco provided a generous grant toward fieldwork expenses, and Mrs. Phyllis Wattis funded the costs of book design and layout. Lastly, my gratitude goes to the numerous village women I met during my travels in Turkey who were willing to share their personal experiences and their knowledge of carpet weaving with an outsider.

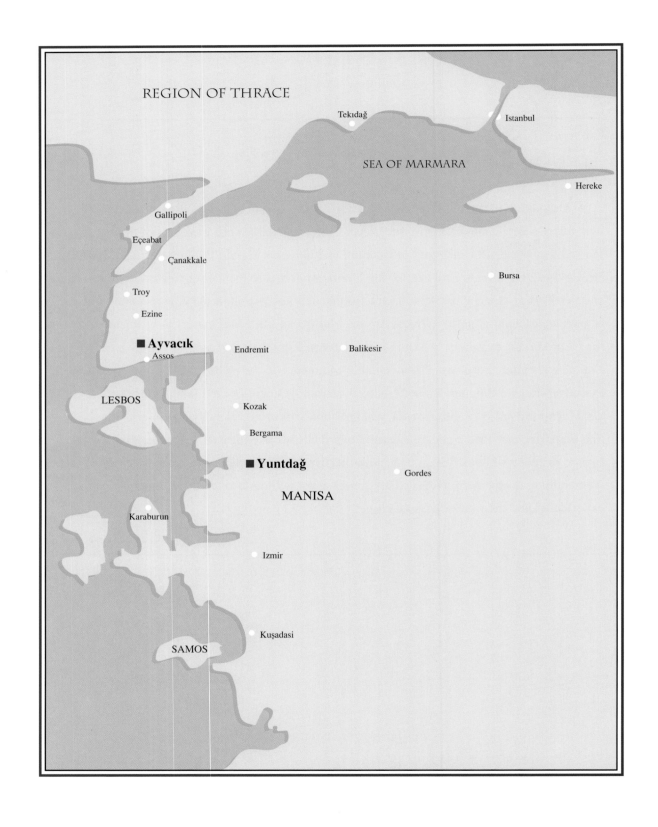

CONTENTS

1. Village carpet from the Ayvacık region in an *altın tabak* (golden plate) design. 1992.
   (Photo Harald Böhmer)

INTRODUCTION

In Turkey, works of art cover the floors. The region has long been known for its carpet-weaving traditions. From nomadic tribal flatweaves and knotted pile carpets to the luxurious silk textiles of the Ottoman court, rich colors and bold geometric designs have expressed the aesthetic heritage of Anatolian people throughout the centuries. Though much has been written on antique carpets and their history, we lack literature on contemporary carpet-weaving in modern-day Anatolia — the Asiatic part of Turkey.

In villages today, very little has changed in the technology of carpet making since its early beginnings; women still use the drop spindle for spinning, and weave on the same type of loom as their ancestors did. Villagers shear the sheep, card the wool, and dye the skeins much as their forebears did in ancient times. These traditional folkways have survived to this day, an unbroken link with the past.

This book focuses on only one small part of that cultural legacy — woollen pile carpets handknotted by village women in the Aegean region of western Turkey. Our story concerns a carpet-weaving project called DOBAG, acronym for *Doğal Boya Araştırma ve Geliştirme Projesi* — the Natural Dye Research and Development Project — supervised by Marmara University in Istanbul. Established in 1981, the project successfully reintroduced natural dye methods in carpet-making villages and revitalized an indigenous textile art. Our story is about people as well as carpets, people reclaiming part of their artistic heritage, men and women striving for self-sufficiency and regaining their traditional means of livelihood through the establishment of two carpet-weaving cooperatives, and the project's effect on the pattern of village life, especially for the weavers and their families.

My involvement with the DOBAG project began in 1990 while I was working as Folk Arts Coordinator in the Anthropology Department at the California Academy of Sciences — San Francisco's natural history museum. Working primarily within the local community, I conducted ethnographic fieldwork in urban neighborhoods to identify folk artists to participate in the museum's Traditional Arts Program — an ongoing series of weekly presentations of ethnic music, dance, and crafts.

That summer I received a phone call from Michael Scott, manager of Return to Tradition — a gallery and retail outlet for handmade carpets produced by the DOBAG cooperatives. He explained that two village women would be coming to San Francisco later that year to provide weaving demonstrations in the downtown store. He suggested that the Academy take advantage of this opportunity and include the weavers in the Traditional Arts Program along with an exhibit of about seventy carpets.

This marked the beginning of a long and happy relationship between the Academy and the carpet-weaving villages of western Turkey. The weavers arrived in the museum in November 1990, set up looms, demonstrated their skills daily for one week, interacted with the American public with the help of an interpreter, and generally impressed museum staff and visitors alike with their warm personalities and their willingness to share this aspect of their culture with others.

Since then, two weavers have returned annually, some for repeat visits, others new to the experience of leaving husband and children, traveling on a plane halfway around the world, eating unusual food, and meeting people from backgrounds very different from their own.

That first visit, in 1990, was unforgettable. The museum's main floor came alive with a panoply of richly colored and visually exciting carpets — a feast for the eyes. Carpets covered the floor, hung from the walls, and lay across benches. Academy visitors appreciated and enjoyed the soft textures, brilliant colors, and complex designs. Initially enamored of the textiles as art objects, I found my interest gradually shifting from the carpets to their makers. The women sparked my curiosity, and I resolved to learn the significance of carpet weaving in their daily lives.

In the presentation of live folk-art programs in a museum setting, the art form is taken from its original context in the community and set into an artificial milieu. Traditional music, dance, and crafts endure from one generation to the next because they are relevant to the daily or ceremonial life of a particular folk group, and express and validate cultural identity. Brought into a museum and placed in the spotlight, the function changes: Folk art becomes theater — contrived performance, staged before an audience of outsiders for their education and entertainment. Far from home, it is far removed from its meaningful sociocultural niche.

So it was with the Turkish weavers. I had seen the carpets and met the women; now I wanted to experience carpet weaving on its own terms — in the villages of western Turkey. On my first visit, in 1992, I flew to Istanbul, a city of minarets and mosques. To whet my appetite, I sought out modern carpets for sale in the Grand Bazaar and pored over Selçuk carpets from the thirteenth century on exhibit in the Museum of Turkish and Islamic Art and the Vakıflar Museum.

My friend, Linda Robinson, a long-time resident of Istanbul and assistant to the DOBAG project, joined me to act as interpreter and we set off by bus, traveling through the region of Thrace, along the Sea of Marmara, and into the Gallipoli Peninsula. Leaving Europe behind, we crossed the Dardanelles on the Eceabat ferry, bound for the harbor town of Çanakkale. Now on the Asian side, we continued south, skirting the archaeological site of ancient Troy, to arrive at Ayvacık — a central location for carpet-producing villages. It was springtime, with sheep shearing in full swing, the fields ablaze with wild flowers, and the weather warm and dry. We visited the annual Ayvacık fair and watched goat bells being hammered into shape from sheets of copper; we sampled regional dishes in Ereçek, rode camels near Süleymanköy, haggled for handcrotched lace in coastal Assos, and bounced over bumpy roads from one village to the next, observing and absorbing the rhythm of daily life and, importantly, visiting the weavers' homes and meeting their families. These memorable experiences are part of this book.

The DOBAG project is many things — a social and economic experiment, a return to the traditional methods of natural dyeing, a renaissance of hand-crafted textiles, an attempt at cultural conservation. Above all, it is the story of village women continuing to weave carpets and create works of art as their grandmothers did before them.

2. Cennet Deneri demonstrates carpet weaving at the
California Academy of Sciences, 1994. (Photo Charlotte Fiorito)

REVITALIZATION

Our story began in Istanbul in 1960. Dr. Harald Böhmer, a German chemist from Delmenhorst, near Bremen, had recently arrived in the city on a seven-year contract to teach chemistry, physics, and biology in the German High School. Quickly becoming an unabashed Turkophile, Dr. Böhmer was fascinated with all that Turkey had to offer. He studied Turkish history and culture, learned the language, and soon became interested in the colorful antique carpets in Istanbul's museums. By comparison, the contemporary carpets he saw on sale in the Grand Bazaar struck him as ugly and lifeless.

At the end of his teaching contract, Böhmer and his family moved back to Germany, returning to Istanbul in 1974 for a second posting. By now his interest in Turkish carpets, their designs, and colors had developed into a passion. He especially admired a certain shade of golden yellow found in the antique carpets but not present in the modern rugs in the covered bazaar. Dr. Böhmer and his wife, Renate, who shared her husband's enthusiasm for Turkish carpets, noticed other color differences between old and new carpets. The modern versions seemed garish and discordant, whereas the brilliance of antique colors harmonized.

The visual difference stemmed from the dyes. Synthetic or so-called aniline dyes, available in Turkey since the 1860s, had gradually replaced organic dyes in handmade carpets. Böhmer decided to investigate the sources of the original dyes. Unfortunately there was little written documentation on the subject of Anatolian dyes, and in the villages knowledge of dye plants, once orally transmitted from one generation to the next, had been lost over time.

In 1976 Böhmer learned of a new laboratory technique called thin-layer chromatography (TLC), devised by a chemist, Dr. Helmut Schweppe, that allows minute particles of fibers from antique textiles to be examined without damaging the fabric. Previously used in the analysis of fragile Coptic textiles, the TLC process separates chemical substances in solution. Thus the components that make up a particular dye can be isolated and identified. With a grant from the German Research Society (Deutsche Forschungsgemeinschaft), Böhmer set up a makeshift laboratory in his kitchen. With the cooperation of Dr. Nazan Ölçer, the director of the Museum of Turkish and Islamic Art, Dr. Böhmer analyzed the dyes in rugs of all ages from the museum's collections. Professor Oktay Aslanapa of Istanbul University also assisted Dr. Böhmer by convincing other museums throughout Turkey to make their carpet collections available for scientific analysis. After analyzing more than two hundred carpets, Böhmer compared the results with those of known vegetable dyes and was able to match the dyes with plants indigenous to Turkey. As some plants have a limited geographic distribution and were used only locally for dyeing, Böhmer's botanical research, supported by Professor Hüsnü Demiriz from Istanbul University, enabled him to trace the regional origin of certain antique rugs by identifying their dye sources.

During their travels around Anatolia, Harald and Renate Böhmer continued to wonder why village weavers readily accepted the new synthetic dyes when every other stage of carpet making from spinning to weaving remained conservative and true to tradition. What were the advantages of chemical dyes over natural ones, to make villagers abandon plant dyes?

In 1856 an English research assistant, William Henry Perkin, while trying to synthesize quinine, had accidently discovered a new coal-tar dye, which he called mauveine. From his pioneering work, the synthetic dye industry was established throughout the world, with Germany taking the lead in experimentation and standardization. By the turn of the century, hundreds of synthetic dyes were patented. Cheaper to produce than natural dyes, they could be processed in large quantities and took less time to make and use. They were ideal for the mass-production of factory textiles. In the 1880s synthetic dyes invaded Turkey's carpet-weaving centers and cottage industries.

In Anatolia, carpets have always been a trade commodity, woven for export as well as for home consumption. Eleventh-century Crusaders were probably the first to carry Oriental carpets to Europe on their return home. Documents from 1492 record the export of Turkish rugs to Italy, evidenced by the depiction of Turkish carpets in European paintings from the fifteenth century (Raby 1986:29-38). During the nineteenth century there was increased demand for handmade carpets among the new European middle classes. Suddenly all things Oriental had become fashionable, stimulated by a series of international expositions held in London, Paris, and Vienna between 1851 and 1876. Western-ers viewed the East as mysterious and exotic, fueled by the popular tales of *A Thousand and One Nights*.

Previously, Oriental carpets were only to be found in the homes of the nobility, but with the emergence of the monied bourgeoisie, consumer demand outstripped supply, and rug prices increased. For the villagers, collecting and processing plants into dyes was labor intensive and time consuming. By comparison, chemical dyes made work faster and cheaper. To speed up manufacture and keep city dealers well supplied, weavers switched to chemical dyes.

Aniline dyes were sold in packets or small tins with written instructions for use. At that time, most villagers did not receive a formal education, so were unable to read the labels. Mistakes were made, resulting in yarns prone to color fading and bleeding. Moreover, villagers could only afford to buy the cheapest, poor-quality dyes available in local shops.

Even the literate weaver was faced with a further difficulty. Dye recipes called for accuracy. Exact amounts of each color had to be measured in milli-grams to get the required hue and villagers did not own the necessary measuring apparatus. Unable to control dye ratios, weavers simply could not faith-fully reproduce the colors of their traditional palette from commercial dyes. Thus, many factors contrib-uted to the decline in quality of the finished carpet.

There was also an obvious visual difference between the synthetic and natural dyes. With aniline dyes, color combinations in the woven carpet appeared to clash, to grate on the nerves, whereas natural dyes produced subtleties of hue and blended together harmoniously. This difference is attributed to our sensory perception — the human eye's ability to register reflected light and convey it via the optical nerve to the brain as an assigned color. Natural dyes are reflected differently from synthetic substances. Color is literally in the eye of the beholder.

When placed side by side, threads of red, blue, and yellow synthetic dyes appear discordant and loud. The same three primary colors in natural dyes — madder red, indigo blue, and chamomile yellow — appear softer and combine well when placed together. The answer lies in the impurities in natural dyestuffs. A dye such as madder red contains small amounts of the other two primary colors, and therefore reflects trace elements of blue and yellow as well as the predominant red. The brain registers these differ-ences, the presence of all three primary colors within each natural dye causing the harmonizing effect and making it impossible to create bad color combinations with naturally dyed yarn.

Synthetic dyes, in contrast, are pure color. Some people prefer the bright, vibrant colors of chemical dyes; others find them monotonous and harsh. The nineteenth-century middle-class consumer, who desired handmade carpets to match the living room decor, generally preferred the mellow look of antique carpets. This was easily accomplished. To suit Western tastes, dealers doctored aniline-dyed carpets to subdue the bright colors and age them artificially, producing fake antiques. Finishing treatments included immersion in caustic bleach solutions and clipping the black wool in a design to simulate the effects of corrosion. (In genuine antique rugs, once-black areas are often missing because the chemicals in black dye eat away at the wool over time.)

George Lewis provides a vivid description of the doctoring process. "For toning down the bright colors, they use chloride of lime, oxalic acid, or lemon juice; for giving them an old appearance they use coffee grounds, and for an artificial sheen or luster the rugs are usually run between hot rollers after the application of glycerine or paraffin wax; they are sometimes buried in the ground for a time, and water color paints are frequently used to restore the color in spots where the acid has acted too vigorously" (1920:24). In an earlier account of carpet antiquing, "the rug was plastered with a mixture of mud, lime and sulphuric acid and then rolled up until the mordants did their work" (Hunter 1906:334). Even without such treatments, many of the early synthetic dyes faded rapidly, becoming washed out and gray — a color not found in the traditional palette.

Discerning rug collectors were mostly aware of the pitfalls of carpet buying. McCoy Jones, an avid collector who donated his entire collection of over five hundred antique rugs to the De Young Museum in San Francisco in 1981, expressed his feelings when interviewed by a local reporter: "What's wrong with modern rugs? Plenty. The whole market has gone to hell. The dyes are very bad, for two reasons. First, the earlier dyes would run. Now they have dyes that don't run anymore, but they're very brash and hard." Jones continued with an anecdote about his Airedale terrier, Hepzibah, and a rug he once bought from a dealer that looked painted. "This dog lies down on this rug and starts licking the border. The dog went on licking the rug and, sure enough, it was white paint. Somebody had painted the rug" (Blum 1981).

Not all carpet-producing countries welcomed synthetic dyes. To protect their industry, the Persian government enacted a law in 1903 forbidding the importation of chemical dyes, and seized and destroyed all fabrics in which they were used. "It was also decreed that a dyer found guilty of using them would have his right hand cut off. The government has never been very strict in enforcing this law, else there would be at the present time many one-handed men in Persia" (Lewis 1920:23).

Nevertheless, not just new dyes and color differences were affecting the quality of commercial village carpets in Anatolia during the past one hundred years. Carpet weaving had changed in other ways too, moving out of the home, where the individual chose the colors and designs, into organized workshops where management controlled the aesthetics.

Women who wove commercial carpets at home to supplement family incomes sold their wares at weekly town markets or annual regional fairs to a middleman. Through a network of dealers, the merchandise arrived at the big bazaars in Izmir and Istanbul for distribution overseas. With the increased demand from foreign markets, dealers were keen to bolster their output and established local ateliers, hiring young girls to work for a daily wage. Grossly underpaid, many weavers felt exploited as cheap labor.

Increasingly, the market came under the control of European entrepreneurs who moved into weaving centers such as Izmir and set up their own workshops, often hiring Greek and Armenian knotters. According to Donald Quataert, who conducted extensive research on social history in the Ottoman archives (Başbakanlık Arşivi) in Istanbul, a similar situation existed in Uşak in the 1890s; to double production, men were hired to spin and dye wool, allowing the women more time for knotting. And in Kula and Gördes, men as well as women wove carpets. "To allow work to extend into the night, the knotters wore miners' helmets, the oil lamps casting the necessary light to allow work to continue" (1986:28-31).

To accommodate the whims of fashion and the decorative tastes of consumers, merchants stipulated the colors and designs, as well as provided the looms and machine-spun wool. Weavers copied designs in the form of cartoons (örnek) or diagrammatic instructions, and were not allowed to improvise or deviate from the pattern. Women had become mechanical robots rather than creative artisans. This type of manufacture boosted factory profits, and village women selling their carpets at local markets had to drop their prices to compete for sales.

The final blow to village carpet weaving came with the development of the mechanized weaving industry in Turkey in the 1960s. Owning a machine-made carpet became a sign of affluence in Turkey and, for a while, the appeal of handmade carpets declined. Factory production soared, but by 1978

5

some of the large companies had declared bankruptcy because of the saturated market (Powell 1987).

National markets for handwoven carpets dwindled. With sales erratic, dealers bought fewer and fewer village rugs, and paid less and less. To compete with cheaper mass-produced carpets, villagers kept their prices down by using poor quality dyes and wool, and tying fewer knots per square inch to reduce time and swell total output. As workmanship suffered, the consequence was a handwoven carpet of inferior grade that proved barely marketable, further hastening the demise of commercial carpet making at the village level.

Anatolian village women have always produced carpets for their own use — for home furnishings, for a young girl's dowry, and for the customary gift to the local mosque as a memorial to a deceased family member. Prized for their beauty, carpets also represent accummulated wealth and financial security, kept as insurance against unexpected hardship. Thus, economics has always been a factor in carpet making.

By the late 1970s, even those carpets made for home consumption had succumbed to the effects of synthetic dyes and deterioration in quality. Moreover, villagers now acquired machine-made rugs for their homes, a situation pervasive in carpet-weaving areas outside Anatolia as well. While traveling in Iran in 1974, James Opie witnessed two women haggling with a dealer over a rug they wanted to buy. Edging close to see the rug they had happily bought, he found to his surprise that they had bargained for a Belgian machine-made cotton rug. "When for themselves they begin to choose the cheapest and coarsest that western machines can manufacture, then the heart of their tradition must already be gone. This is a great loss for them, and for us" (1981:ix).

In Turkish villages, the art of natural dyeing and the weavers' traditional palette had vanished. Something else was missing, something intangible. The Anatolian carpet had lost its integrity and, with it, its soul. This was the plight that dismayed Harald and Renate Böhmer on their return to Istanbul in 1974.

Having identified the plant sources for natural dyes, Harald Böhmer saw no reason why carpets should not return to their former glory, to the rich chromatic spectrum that existed in former times. But he still faced the problem of reconstructing the dyeing process. Scant literature existed, and those recipes he did find in old books often proved to be full of errors when he tried to duplicate them. On their visits to the countryside, the Böhmers met a few old people who vaguely remembered collecting plants as children but none could recall how to extract dye from the plants. The lore of natural dying appeared to be completely lost.

However, before investigation could continue Böhmer had another, more pressing hurdle to jump. His teaching contract expired in 1979. To remain in Turkey and continue his work on dyestuffs, he sought help from the German Ministry for Economic Cooperation in Bonn, which agreed within the framework of the German Development Service to support his work in Turkey as a German civil servant abroad. But he needed to find permanent employment with an organization sympathetic to his research and which shared his vision of teaching village weavers to use plant dyes. He began the frustrating task of looking for a job. Eventually the State School for Applied Fine Arts in Istanbul agreed to administer the dye research project, which became known as DOBAG, hiring Dr. Böhmer as principal adviser in 1981. In 1982 the school became the Faculty of Fine Arts at Mamara University, with Professor Mustafa Aslier initially heading the DOBAG committee, a position later assumed by Professor Erol Eti, the present dean of the Faculty. The project also received support from the Turkish Forest Ministry.

Once established, the DOBAG project defined its goals: To put into practice Böhmer's research on natural dyes by teaching dyeing methods in selected villages, and to form a self-financing cooperative to market the "new" carpets. The subsequent goal was to revitalize and conserve traditional carpet making and, with strict quality controls, restore the integrity of the craft. Moreover, a retail commodity would supplement family incomes and improve economic conditions in impoverished areas. To promote self-

3. The DOBAG palette of colors.
Süleymanköy 1994.

sufficiency, villagers themselves would make up the membership of the cooperative.

The head of the Forestry Department in the Ayvacık district in western Turkey had heard about DOBAG and, looking for ways to keep local people gainfully employed, he soon contacted Böhmer and his colleagues. The Ayvacık area has a long and unbroken weaving tradition and still maintains the old village designs. Some of the oldest and most famous Turkish carpets known as Ezine and Çanakkale take their names from market towns in the region. But by the 1980s even these once-admired carpets had deteriorated in quality, the old colors long replaced by synthetic substitutes. It seemed an ideal location to initiate the DOBAG experiment.

First the dye recipes had to be reconstructed. Böhmer and his wife set about reinventing the dyer's craft. With a great deal of imagination and a lot of trial and error, they devised recipes suitable for conditions in the villages. For example, the indigo dyeing process relies on the strict control of acidity and temperature. To simplify the procedure for home dyeing, small pellets of glue readily available in village markets were added to the dye bath to obtain the desired results. The commonplace tulip-shaped Turkish tea glass was used as a standard measuring cup. By 1981, the Böhmers had mastered the full range of traditional colors — all except violet, which revealed its secret later.

Before the Böhmers could reintroduce home dyeing methods in selected villages, they had to establish rapport with the weavers — conservative village women not accustomed to making eye contact with men. At that time, in the early 1980s, some women still veiled their faces. Mrs. Böhmer spent months in the villages, gaining the women's confidence. Eventually the weavers accepted the husband-and-wife team in their midst.

The first dyeing demonstration took place in the village of Çınarpınar, south of Ezine in the province of Çanakkale. In the scorching hot summer months, the Böhmers held open-air seminars and distributed simple step-by-step recipes with illustrated instructions. Villagers cooperated eagerly, weaving a small carpet for test marketing in Istanbul — the first naturally dyed rug to be made in the area for generations. By the end of the year, twenty families had made twenty old-style carpets. The vision of Harald and Renate Böhmer was realized.

4a. Renate Böhmer discussing plant dyes with villagers.
The man holding the dried madder root knows the plant as a weed
in the cotton fields but is unaware that it yields red dye.
Yuntdağ 1981. (Photo Harald Böhmer)

4b. Harald Böhmer
supervises indigo dyeing.
Süleymanköy 1997.
(Photo Harald Böhmer)

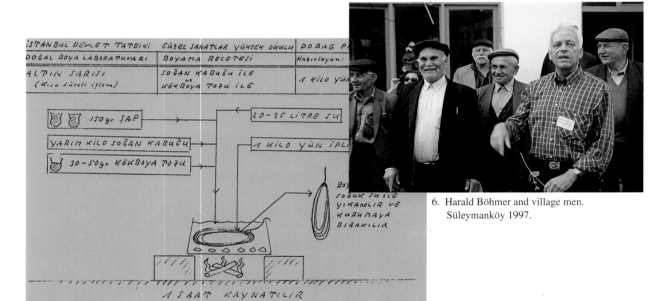

6. Harald Böhmer and village men.
   Süleymanköy 1997.

5. Simple step-by-step dye recipes were distributed to villagers in 1981.
   (Photo Harald Böhmer)

THE COOPERATIVE TAKES SHAPE

With the successful reintroduction of natural dyes in the Ayvacık region, the stage was set for the next phase of the DOBAG project — the formation of a village cooperative to market the carpets. Such an endeavor required outside funding. Fortunately the provincial governor, Nurettin Turan, was farsighted enough to see the long-term benefits to local villagers and was keen to support the project. He petitioned the federal government for a loan of nearly $100,000 to finance the start up. Six months later the money arrived from Ankara and the struggling Ayvacık cooperative was in business. (Within six years this capital was all repaid.)

7. Süleymanköy 1994.

8. Assos 1992.

Known as Troas in ancient times, the Ayvacık district is situated in the Aegean Peninsula, an area rich in history and strewn with the ruins of ancient civilizations. On the coast, the reconstructed columns of the temple to Athena, originally built in the sixth century B.C., look out to sea from above the mountain village of Assos. Inland, the Hellenistic city of Pergamum, a photographer's dream, now bustles with as many tourists as it once did with successive Greek and Roman citizens.

The site of legendary Troy, immortalized by Homer in his epic poem *The Iliad*, is less than an hour away by car from the town of Ayvacık. Commanding a strategic hilltop position at the mouth of the Dardanelles Straits, Troy no longer threatens the trading ships of ancient Greece seeking access to the Black Sea. Today, its activities are archaeological. Excavations of the first settlement (3000-2500 B.C.) uncovered spindle whorls and loom weights — evidence that spinning and weaving were established occupations in this area by the Bronze Age.

The Ayvacık district covers 550 square miles, with a total village population of around twenty-eight thousand. The cooperative's distribution center is in the market town of Ayvacık, a community of nearly five thousand. There are seventy-nine surrounding villages with smaller populations. Of these villages, twenty-five participate in the cooperative, the members producing about one thousand carpets a year.

The landscape is beautiful — vineyards and orchards in the valleys, pine forests on the mountain slopes, small cornfields and olive groves, and nestling villages of gray, stone houses in the panoramic distance. On the rocky, barren hillsides roaming flocks of sheep and goats graze on the prickly leaves of buckthorn bushes, shaping them into strange, living sculptures. Bedecked with jingling bells and blue bead amulets, camels tramp the hills, loaded with firewood and charcoal instead of the nomad's tent.

9. Yörük village of Çamkalabak.

10. Ayşe Erçan and granddaughter.
Çamkalabak 1992.

However, overgrazing by sheep and deforestation for firewood have rendered the land agriculturally unproductive. With no factories and only seasonal work, there is scant employment for the men besides herding. In winter villagers pick olives at the coast, and some families augment their incomes by selling beans grown in their gardens.

Local people call themselves either *Yörük* or *Yerli*. The Yörük, meaning "we who roam" or wanderer from the Turkish word *yürümek*, to walk (Acar 1982:20), are once-nomadic tribes who began to settle in the area, voluntarily or by government enforcement, during the nineteenth century, though some groups resisted settlement until as recently as sixty years ago. Yörük is a generic term for an ethnically defined group of people related through paternal lines. There are many subdivisons of Yörük tribes scattered in regions throughout Turkey who call themselves by the old tribal names, such as the Saçıkaralı, Sarıkeçeli, and Tekkeli.

A survey carried out in 1898 along the Aegean Coast lists eighty-eight separate tribal divisions (Landreau and Yohe 1983:18). Those now living in the area around Ayvacık had their winter pasture (*kışla*) where their villages are now situated. The summer pastures, *yaylas*, were in the Kazdağ Mountains, one hundred kilometers east of Ayvaçık.

Today the Yörük accept their sedentary life and entire families no longer migrate, though some shepherds still drive their herds to the old *yaylas* each spring for the summer months. (Fewer than one thousand entirely nomadic families remain in Turkey.)

Yerli, or "settled population," is the word used in the old Ottoman census records. Villagers also use this word to describe themselves. Half of the Yerli villages in the Ayvacık area were settled by Turkish immigrants arriving from the Balkans after the 1850s (Powell 1987).

In 1982, a year after the founding of the Ayvacık cooperative, the project expanded into a second district further south, the Yuntdağ — a mountain range between Manisa and Bergama that reaches altitudes of over three thousand feet. *Yunt* is an old Turkish word meaning horse and *dağ* means mountain; hence, *Yuntdağ* literally translated means the horse mountain or horse mountain country. Visually not unlike the American Rockies, the Yuntdağ's boulders and outcrops conjure up the quintessential Western movie set.

The fifty small villages situated on the slopes and in the valleys of the Yuntdağ will not be found on any map. Some of the houses are one hundred years old, with interiors that clearly reveal the ancestry of their occupants. The woven storage bags (*ala çuval*)

11. The Yuntdağ 1995.

12. The village of Örselli 1996.

13. Interior of village house with woven storage bags
    hanging on walls. Örselli 1995.

filled with flour and grain and arranged in rows along the walls are reminiscent of the furnishings of a nomadic tent.

This stony, barren region, with very little rainfall, supports but a few scattered oaks and wild pistachio trees. The induced settlement of nomads over the past century indirectly contributed to the decline in vegetation in the area. The Yörük form of pastoralism, based on the regular movement of livestock between different climatic zones, is called transhumance. In former times, flocks of sheep were rotated among several pastures with the seasons, but compulsory settlement broke the cyclic rhythm of migrations and proved to be an ecological disaster. Flocks left to graze the same land throughout the year gradually destroyed the forests. Sheep ownership dwindled and, today, village life is precarious. The poor soil makes the terrain unsuitable for crops. Winters are cold and hard, spring is short, and summer is hot and arid. Rivers run dry, springs dry up, and wells and cisterns are the only source of water for man and beast (Böhmer 1989).

Modern highways bypass the Yuntdağ. Horses, camels, and donkeys were the only means of transport until very recently; now gravel roads, power lines, and water pipes connect villages, though the region remains poor and underdeveloped. In the summer families seek work in the plains, harvesting grapes, cotton, and tobacco, and supplement their income picking wild pistachio nuts to sell.

Because of the Yuntdağ's isolation, traditional carpet weaving and other folk art forms have survived with little outside influence, making it an ideal location for the second weaving cooperative. In this district, with five participating villages, the reintroduction of natural dyeing took a different approach. In Ayvacık, dye demonstrations were open to all, and just about everyone in each village learned plant dyeing. In the Yuntdağ, it was decided to train only one dyer per village, who would work for the cooperative and be of service to all the weavers.

14. The village of Sarıahmetli 1995.

15. Handwoven donkey bags have found new uses. Ayvacık 1995.

Another fundamental difference between the two cooperatives lies in the organization of weaving work. In Ayvacık, each weaver supplies all her own tools and materials, and she can sell the finished carpet to the cooperative or elsewhere if she chooses. Some weavers purchase wool from the cooperative, which now owns a modern carding machine. In the Yuntdağ, the cooperative provides all the tools and materials, and pays the weaver for her labor. Regardless of the work system, all weavers have the freedom to make personal choices in the colors and designs of their rugs.

16. Dye house. Örselli 1995.

17. Washed carpets dry in the sun. Örselli 1992.

To get started, the Yuntdağ cooperative needed money to buy looms, dyestuffs, wool, and equipment, as well as for marketing and the construction of a communal dye house. Yuntdağ received a developmental aid grant from the German Agency for Technical Cooperation.

From the outset, villagers operated the cooperatives themselves and took on the responsibility of distribution, thereby eliminating the services of a middleman. In Ayvacık, with two hundred and twenty participating households, it is the men who hold cooperative membership in their own names, and receive payment on behalf of the female weavers in the family. Not all women agree with this system, though it follows society's custom that the man, as head of the house, handle the family's income. Despite cultural convention, times are changing. Now, when a man dies, his widow can take his place as a member, and about twenty women have become members in their own right.

The annual membership fee is about six dollars. At a yearly general meeting, members elect a board of five and the board president is paid a monthly salary. Ayvacık also employs a master dyer, two bookkeepers, one carder, one driver, and three security guards. Registered as a cooperative with the Ministry of Agriculture and Forests, the organization's official title is *Sınırlı Sorumlu Süleyman Köy Tarımsal Kalkınma Kooperatifi.*

The Yuntdağ management differs from that of the Ayvacık cooperative in that the women weavers, rather their husbands, make up the membership, creating the first and only all-female cooperative in Turkey. Hatice Yılmaz, from the village of Örselli, was elected the first woman president in 1989. One hundred and thirty active weavers currently hold membership in their own names. This cooperative is registered with the Ministry for Small Industries as a production and marketing cooperative in which, according to Turkish law, only the producers themselves — in this case, the weavers — can be members. The organization is entitled The Natural Dyed Handwoven Rugs Production and Marketing Cooperative (*Sınırlı Sorumlu Doğal Boyalı Dokumaları Üretim ve Pazarlama Kooperatifi*).

Each cooperative maintains strict quality controls to guarantee high-caliber craftsmanship. Dr. Şerife Atlıhan, a lecturer in textile arts at Marmara University, acts as the cooperative's carpet inspector, visiting each village to check the women's work and also assisting weavers with technical problems. Any rugs not meeting her high standards are rejected. Dr. Atlıhan has worked on the project since 1983 and village women relate easily to her because of similiarities in her background. Her family, like theirs, has a nomadic past and she grew up in a village in southeastern Turkey. After working as a primary school teacher, she received a government grant to complete her academic pursuits.

13

Thus, her origins and her education enable her to work well with village weavers.

Each DOBAG carpet is registered at Marmara University and is sold with an attached leather tag guaranteeing that the carpet is dyed with natural dyes, has an authentic Turkish village pattern (rather than a copy of a Caucasian or Persian design), and is not "beautified" in any way with rinsings, bleaches, or other chemical mutilations to give the appearance of an antique. The buyer also gets a certificate recording the weaver's name, her village, the date of manufacture, and the total number of knots in the piece. These identification tags ensure that inferior rugs resembling DOBAG rugs are not mistaken for the genuine article in the marketplace.

The cooperatives maintain standards of pricing to ensure that weavers are fairly compensated. Because of this, the project has met stiff resistance from dealers who have a vested interest in its failure and would like to eliminate the competition. A weaver receives payment based on the number of knots in her carpet, not its size. Additionally, at the end of the fiscal year, the cooperative's annual profits are paid out to the weavers. For each carpet sold on the export market, the weaver receives a further seventy percent of the profit. For instance, in 1989, after deducting four percent of the total profit to finance research and international promotion through Marmara University, the cooperatives distributed $200,000 among the weavers .

DOBAG carpets are made exclusively for export to authorized outlets and are shipped directly from the villages. Currently, the cooperative maintains foreign distribution centers in San Francisco, Oslo, Copenhagen, Bonn, and Perth, and supplies carpets to selected dealers in Oxford, London, Dublin, and Oldenburg.

The project has gained international recognition through numerous magazine articles, exhibits, symposia, and lectures by Dr. Böhmer and his associates. In 1992 the cooperatives received a substantial grant for the purchase of five looms from Aid to Artisans — a Connecticut-based agency that supports craft production throughout the world.

DOBAG leather tag.

Weavers continue to travel annually to the United States and Norway to give educational and promotional demonstrations of carpet weaving. The first major exhibit of DOBAG carpets took place in Wissenschaftszentrum (Science Center) in Bonn in 1982 and, since 1990, the California Academy of Sciences in San Francisco has featured DOBAG carpets in a special exhibit every November. The carpets have also been displayed in galleries and museums in Switzerland, Austria, Germany, the United States (at the World Bank in Washington, D.C.), Ireland, England, Japan, and the United Emirates.

Today the two cooperatives are healthy, successful businesses. In both the Ayvacık and Yuntdağ districts there is a waiting list of families eager to join, but there are no plans to increase membership or expand into other regions of Turkey.

Dr. Böhmer is still involved with the project as technical adviser and continues to supervise research on ancient dyes in the Laboratory for Natural Dyes at Marmara University, where controlling the dyes in DOBAG carpets is an ongoing task. In 1990 he and his colleagues, Dr. Nevin Enez and Dr. Recep Karadağ, analyzed the red-dyed wool in

18. Emine Güler proudly displays her carpet.
    Ayvacık 1996.

19. Cennet Deneri removes her finished carpet from
    the loom. California Academy of Sciences 1995.
    (Photo Dong Lin)

the world's oldest pile carpet — the Pazyryk carpet in the collections of the Hermitage Museum in St. Petersburg, Russia. Excavated in 1947, the carpet fragment had been preserved for twenty-five hundred years in the ice of Siberia. The laboratory investigates Old World insect dyes as well as plant dyes, and recently rediscovered in Anatolia such dye insects as Ararat kermes *(Porphyrophora hameli)* and Mediterranean kermes *(Kermes vermilio)*.

DOBAG rugs now adorn the walls and floors of homes and museums worldwide. International demand is high, reinforcing Dr. Böhmer's initial belief that a return to tradition would produce a marketable carpet and that the foreign customer was not too jaded to appreciate the all-natural handmade object. A further appeal for buyers is knowing that the entire process of carpet production takes place in the village and that their purchases directly benefit the weavers.

Once again village families are collecting plants and processing dyes. Every stage of manufacture has the imprint of the human hand, but villagers have also

learned new skills in marketing and distribution, becoming astute businessmen and women. Regular employment has improved living conditions for weavers' families and brought a degree of prosperity to poor areas without disrupting the social structure and traditional way of life. The DOBAG project also transformed the marketplace; like an infectious virus, the return to natural dyes spread from village to village, causing a minor revolution within the Turkish carpet industry.

The carpets speak for themselves — alive with colors that glow and harmonize, breathing with resurrected family designs woven from memory, and born of the weaver's new-found confidence in her work. In fitting tribute to all that the cooperatives signify, DOBAG carpets have been dubbed "tomorrow's antiques."

MAKING A VILLAGE CARPET

Made entirely from wool, the village carpet begins life on the rocky hillsides of the Aegean Peninsula where flocks of sheep roam and graze as they have since prehistoric times, their tinkling copper neckbells in musical harmony.

Village sheep are one of many fat-tailed breeds indigenous to Anatolia that thrive in arid climates. When food is scarce, they survive on the fat stored in their abnormally large tails. The animals supply meat and milk as well as a fine, lustrous fleece — the raw material for the handspun yarn.

Although weaving is women's work, the men of the household contribute in many ways to the manufacture of a carpet, starting with the skills of animal husbandry. During the hot summer months, the men tend the sheep at night when it is cool, sleeping during the day or socializing in the village tea house, the *kahve*. In winter the shepherd is warmly wrapped in the traditional cape of white felted wool, the *kepenek*, which is windproof, waterproof, and doubles as a sleeping bag at night. In the high barren areas where the cold winter winds sweep across the plateau, circular stone shelters dot the landscape, built to protect both sheep and herders.

20. Anatolian fat-tailed sheep with shepherd wearing the traditional felted *kepenek*. Yuntdağ 1981. (Photo Harald Böhmer)

21. On the high plateau, circular stone shelters protect sheep and herders from the harsh elements. Ayvacık area 1992.

It is the men who shear the sheep, a job requiring patience, dexterity, and strength, for shearing is slow, laborious work. Armed only with a pair of large scissors *(kırklık)*, the shearer must first hold down the struggling animal, tie its legs together, and proceed to snip off the fleece carefully by hand. The wool from different parts of the sheep's body (the back, the underbelly, and so on) are not sorted, as it is in some areas of the Middle East, but mixed together for spinning.

22. Sheep shearing with *kırklık*. Erecek 1992.

There are two shearings a year, in May and September. The winter wool *(yapağı)*, sheared in the spring, has a long staple (the length measurement of the fiber) and can be heated to boiling temperatures without matting. This wool is suitable for dyeing and eventually becomes the colored yarn used for the knotted pile. (It takes the winter wool of about ten sheep to tie 100,000 knots into a rug measuring about sixteen feet square). However, the winter fleece is badly tangled, greasy, and unevenly stained. It takes time to clean and remove burrs, and half of the total weight may be lost in cleaning. The wool is washed by being pounded with a wooden mallet in running water. Washing also removes some of the natural lanolin, but it is important to leave a small amount in the wool to facilitate spinning and to prevent the spinner's hands from becoming rough and chapped. Too much lanolin adhering to the fibers will repel the dye in places, giving a mottled effect.

The summer wool, sheared in September, has short fibers prone to matting. This wool is left a natural color and is used for the warp threads stretched on the loom, and for the weft threads woven between each row of knots. Summer wool is also ideal for making felt.

Sheep are not communally owned by the village. They are family property, though not every family owns livestock. Some weavers buy their fleeces from other families. The cooperatives also buy good-quality Central Anatolian wool in bulk from dealers in Konya, for resale to the weavers in ten-pound bags.

In preparation for spinning, the wool is carded or combed to arrange the fibers into loose rovings or "rolags" and to remove any remaining dirt. Now the women take over the responsibility of processing the raw wool into yarn. Most women have their own handcarders, although each cooperative now has a carding machine for the weavers' use.

Today, as in the past, women weave carpets for their own family needs. Daughters learn the skills necessary for every stage of carpet production, from carding and spinning to the finished product. Society expects a young woman, in her role as wife and mother, to weave her own dowry and to supply the textile needs of the household. However, carpets are also a source of income and, for cooperative members, it is more economical to have a division of labor and specialization. For example, in each village master dyers are employed as a service to the weavers.

Typically the elderly women, some well into their seventies or eighties, are the designated spinners. After a lifetime of tying carpet knots, and decades of sowing, weeding, and harvesting crops in the fields, their hands become gnarled and susceptible to arthritis, but they can still spin. Although machine-made yarn can be purchased in town stores, weavers prefer to spin their own wool because it produces a loosely twisted yarn that exposes more fibers to the dye, and the irregularities of handspun yarn give it interesting color subtleties in the dyeing process.

Women use two methods of handspinning — a drop spindle *(iğ)* and a spinning wheel *(çıkrık)*. The drop spindle spins a tight, strong yarn that is used for the warp threads *(çözgü)* and the weft *(atkı)*. A simple yet effective device, the drop spindle resembles a spinning top. A wooden stick about fifteen inches in length is centered through a weighted flywheel, or whorl, to sustain the momentum. The diameter and the weight of the whorl can be adapted to create different types of yarn. The drop spindle is used in many other societies worldwide (Navajo weavers in Arizona use the same technique), with whorls fashioned from a variety of materials — wood, stone, ceramics. Villagers in western Turkey carve their whorls from wood. Other design factors are the length of the rod and the whorl's position on the shaft. Western Anatolia is known as a low-whorl area.

When set in motion, the pointed end of the stick rests on the ground. (I have seen Yörük girls anchor the end between their toes.) There are minor variations in other parts of the world: In West Africa, the drop spindle rests in a piece of calabash; in Guatemala, in a bowl. In the Peruvian Andes, women spin while on the move, the suspended spindle rotating freely a few inches from the ground (Hecht 1989:83, 163, 184).

The drop spindle can rotate clockwise or counter-clockwise to produce either a spiral Z-twist or S-twist thread. For Turkish village carpets, the wool is spun in a Z-twist, then two strands are plied together in the opposite direction, forming an S-twist. As the yarn forms, it is wound onto the shaft above the whorl.

17

23. Fatma Ercan uses a drop spindle. Süleymanköy 1992.

24. Rabiye Ercan uses a simple spinning wheel. Çamkalabak 1992.

The drop spindle represents one of the oldest forms of handspinning, and the technology has remained unchanged throughout Anatolian history. Though the wheel spins faster, the drop spindle has survived into the twentieth century because of certain practical advantages. Being light and portable, it was well suited to the nomadic life of tribal weavers, and also allowed spinning to be combined with a host of other domestic activities. While living in the village of Susanoğlu in the Toros Mountains, the ethnographer Anita Landreau observed: "Spinning is incorporated into all phases of daily life. Wherever we went visiting, we carried our spinning and spun as we socialized; after meals we sat around and spun; during breaks from chores, we spun; even when going for walks, we spun as we walked" (Landreau and Yohe 1983:84).

The yarn designated for tying the knots is made on the spinning wheel, which gives a looser twist that enables the dye to penetrate the fibers. The wheel is also used for plying two or more strands of yarn. Fashioned of wood or metal, the wheel is turned by a handle. With one hand, the spinner sets the wheel in motion, cranking the handle, while deftly pulling out fibers from carded batting with her other hand — a true feat of coordination. Similar wheels are used in India, Guatemala, and Indonesia (Hecht 1989:108).

The handspun yarn is now ready for dyeing. Natural dyes fall into three categories defined by method — vat dyes, direct dyes, and mordant dyes. Vat dyes need chemical additives in the dye bath to

25. Emine Güler plying yarn. Süleymanköy 1995.

make the dye soluble by the chemical process of reduction. Direct dyes are applied directly to the fiber without the use of a fixative. The process called mordant dyeing (from the Latin *mordere*, to bite) requires two stages. First the yarn is chemically treated, to enable the dye molecules to bond with the fibers, then it is immersed in the dye bath, to produce colors that are insoluble and lightfast.

Village weavers predominantly use the mordanting method. Wet skeins of yarn are dipped in a hot bath containing metal salts, either alum (potassium aluminum sulfate) or iron (ferrous sulfate), which act as a catalyst. The choice of mordant affects the hue. For example, alum combined with madder root produces a luminous, brilliant red; iron and madder give a duller, russet red. Small quantities of copper salts added to the dye bath act as a mordant and increase the color's resistance to fading. After the skeins are mordanted, they are laid out in the sun or hung up to dry.

Knowledge of dye recipes and plant resources, once common lore passed on orally from one generation to the next, had disappeared when the Böhmers reintroduced the art of natural dyeing in 1981. Weavers experimented with the dye recipes, producing soft muted hues, rich blues and reds, colors that harmonized and unified the carpet designs. Color has become the hallmark of DOBAG carpets.

In many villages, dyeing is now a specialized craft, practiced by a master dyer employed by the cooperative. Currently, about half the weavers dye their own wool and the cooperative's dyer does the rest. Typically, dyeing activities take place in a centrally located area outdoors where the dyes simmer in heavy aluminum pots called *kazan*, set in rows over wood-burning fires. Nearby, dyed skeins hang to dry in the open air.

Powdered natural dyestuffs can now be purchased in neighboring towns, but cooperative members prefer to collect their own plants for processing into dyes. Many dye-yielding plants, which are called generically *kök boya,* or root dye, grow in the region, but only the main ones used in village carpets are mentioned here.

Red dye comes from dried madder root *(Rubia tinctorum)*, coarsely ground in a stone quern, or handmill. One kilo of wool needs about one kilo of roots. Madder plants grow wild, particularly in cotton fields, where the farmers consider it a weed. Madder produces a wide spectrum of hues, from pale apricot and pink to a rich salmon and brownish red depending on the mordant used. When rinsed in water containing oak ash, the color of madder-dyed wool is enhanced.

Madder also yields a special shade of violet found in many of the antique rugs. In 1982 Josephine Powell, an American ethnologist and documentary photographer living in Istanbul, rediscovered the old method for producing this color from madder alone without adding indigo blue. Powell has spent a

lifetime researching Yörük textiles and has been involved with the DOBAG project from the beginning. Her ideas and technical help proved invaluable in reconstructing some of the dye recipes. Her recipe for violet is one of DOBAG's trade secrets, guarded from competitors in much the same way as the master dyers of an earlier age protected their recipes.

Blue comes from the leaves of the indigo plant *(Isatis tinctoria)*, also known as dyer's woad, which still grows wild in parts of Turkey. The villagers, however, use synthetic indigo, which is chemically identical to natural indigo. This is the only manufactured dye used in DOBAG carpets. Indigo is a vat dye needing a chemical agent that, by reduction, actually turns the blue indigo powder into a soluble yellow substance. This provides an entertainment in the dyeing process. Watching the dyer lift the skeins from the hot liquid, we see bright yellow magically turn to blue within seconds, the result of oxidization when the dye is exposed to the air.

In Anatolia there is only one red-producing plant and one blue-producing plant (madder and indigo). About twenty different plants yield shades of yellow. Most grow wild, though some families now cultivate dyer's weld *(Reseda luteola)* in garden plots. Yellow also comes from the blossoms of wild chamomile *(Anthemis chia)*, which contains the dye apigenin, from the flowers of the ox-eye chamomile *(Anthemis tinctoria)*, which contain the dye isorhamnetin, from sumac *(Cotinus coggrygia)*, or wig-shrub, which contains the dye fisetin, and from spurge *(Euphorbia biglandulosa)*, which contains the dye quercetin, to name but a few yellow producing plants.

No dye plant yields a fast and intense green. This color results from two separate dyeings; first indigo blue, then yellow from weld. The same applies to orange; first chamomile yellow, then madder red. Brown dye is an extract of walnut pods *(Juglans regia)* used as a direct dye on wool fibers without a mordant. Many of the old tribal rugs have naturally brown wool from goats, sheep, and camels.

Black dye comes from plants with a high tannic acid content, such as the oak apples, acorn cups, and bark of the knobbly oak *(Quercus macrolepis*

26. Collecting chamomile
    for yellow dye.
    Ayvacık 1981.
    (Photo Harald Böhmer)

27. Prepared chamomile, madder, and dyer's weld
    are ready for adding to the dye pots.

28. Dried madder root.
29. Grinding madder root with a stone mill.
    (Photo Harald Böhmer)

30. Yarn is dyed in large pots over wood-burning fires.
Süleymanköy 1992.

31. Hasan Sezer, master dyer, demonstrates that indigo dye
is transformed from yellow to blue on oxidization.
Süleymanköy 1992.

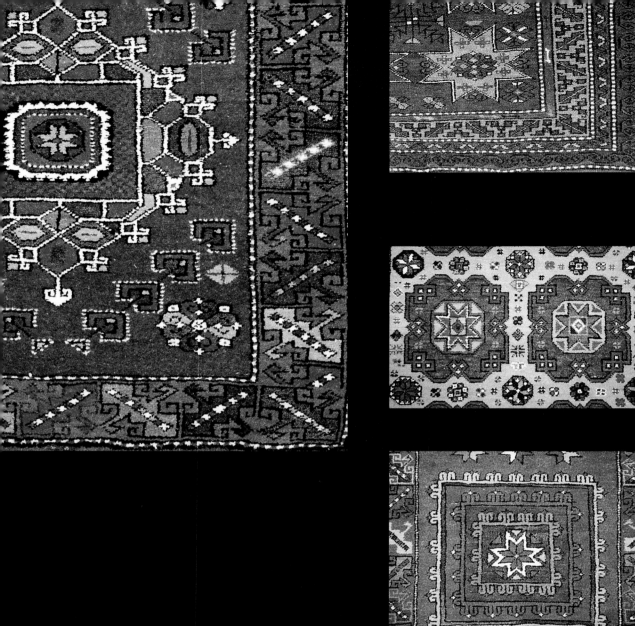
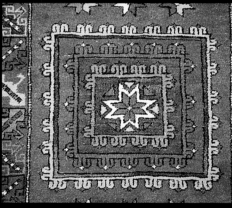

Kotschy), also called the Walloon oak, and pomegranate skins *(Punica granatum)*, as well as the leaves of a shrub, dyer's sumac *(Rhus coriaria)*, used with an iron mordant. (For further information on natural dyes, see Böhmer and Bruggemann 1983:88-117.)

Plant dyes rarely produce uniform batches of colored yarn as do aniline dyes. In the dyeing process, a host of variables comes into play, factors that can alter the hue in subtle and unexpected ways, such as slight changes in the temperature of the dye bath, the choice of mordant, the quantity of dyestuff in the bath, the pH of the water, irregularities in the twist of the yarn, the amount of lanolin in the fibers, or the length of time they are immersed in the hot dye. In the finished carpet, these elements of chance create an interesting tonal variety, a visual effect called *abrash*. It is these color irregularities, these nuances of shade, that many find attractive in the Turkish village carpet.

In contrast, the accurate and controlled process of industrially manufactured dyes reproduces the same color consistently and reliably. These dyes are ideal for mass-producing yard upon yard of identically colored yarn in textile factories. Some people prefer the near-perfect evenness of synthetic color; others perceive them as flat and monotonous. It's a matter of individual taste.

With the wool spun and the yarn dyed, the next step is warping the loom — a critical stage in production, for the warp is the foundation on which the carpet takes shape. A communal, outdoor activity, warping takes three experienced women between four and five hours to complete. Without any mechanical measuring device, weavers estimate the length of the warp and drive two wooden stakes into the ground at this distance apart. Alternatively, women may use an apparatus consisting of a long plank with two adjustable poles that can span any length of warp. Walking back and forth, one woman wraps the yarn continuously around the posts while the other

women, one stationed at each post, insert twine between each warp thread, making sure that the stretched threads are in sequence. When the required number is reached, they slide the warp off the posts onto thinner rods that will be lashed onto the warp beams of the loom.

The vertical loom *(iştar* or *tezgah)* is an enormous, heavy contraption constructed of solid, rough-hewn wood and ropes. It is a rectangular frame made of two parallel uprights, or "trees," supporting two horizontal roller beams — the upper warp beam and the lower cloth beam — that hold the warp threads under tension. Protruding wooden levers unlock the roller beams so they can turn freely and allow finished sections of the carpet to be rolled onto the lower cloth beam. Thus, the weaver remains level with her work without needing to adjust her sitting position. Recently the cooperatives purchased a quantity of metal looms, ranging in price from $200 to $500 each depending on size, which have the advantage of keeping the warp at a consistent tension because the loom parts do not break or bend.

In the summer, weavers set up their looms under a porch or lean-to attached to the house. In winter, weaving takes place indoors. Traditional houses have one small window per room, making the work areas extremely dark. Frequently women weave by the light of an open door or place the loom directly across the window, creating a framed silhouette against the natural light. The rhythmic twang of fingers plucking warp strings — a soft and soothing music — enhances the scene.

23

32. The traditional palette of natural dyes sets DOBAG carpets apart from their synthetic cousins.

33. Preparing the warp. Süleymanköy 1995.

34. In summer, Fatma Ergün sets up her loom in a porch area. Süleymanköy 1992.

35. The *taban* lever releases the lower beam, the *burgu* lever releases the top beam, to slacken the warp for rolling.

24

36. When working indoors, weavers often place the loom in front of a window for natural light. Çamkalabak 1992.

37. Balls of wool hang from the top of the loom, ready for use. Sarıahmetli 1995.

Turkish carpets fall into two categories defined by weaving technique — knotted pile carpets *(halı)* and flatweaves, the latter often referred to generically as *kilims*. Flatweaving predates pile techniques, being the basic warp and weft structure on which knots are added. As organic matter rarely survives in archaeological sites, there are few extant examples of early weavings. We know that the art of carpet knotting was well established by 500 B.C. — the date attributed to the oldest surviving pile weave, a fragment known as the Pazyryk carpet, made with the symmetrical or so-called Turkish knot. In 1947, the Soviet archaeologist, S. I. Rudenko, and his team, working in the Pazyryk region of the Altai Mountains in Siberia, discovered the carpet fragment among the funerary accoutrements of a Scythian prince in a burial mound. Water seeping into the tomb had frozen, protecting the fabric from decay and aging (Böhmer and Thompson 1991:30-36).

Some believe that the pile technique was brought from Central Asia by nomadic Oğuz Turkmen tribes who began their westward migrations into Anatolia toward the end of the tenth century, settling in sporadic groups throughout the plateau and gradually adopting Islam (Acar 1982:20-22). The double, symmetrical knot in Anatolian carpets is also called the Gördes knot, named after the town of Gördes in western Anatolia. Colored yarn is actually wrapped, not knotted, around two adjacent warp threads and

snipped off to form the pile. To strengthen the structure of the fabric, two rows of plain weft follow each row of knots. The symmetrical knot forms a robust, hardwearing fabric suitable for functional textiles whereas the single, asymmetrical Persian or Senneh knot lends itself to decorative weavings with refined design details and accurately rendered motifs.

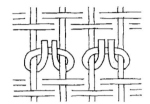

The Turkish symmetrical double knot.

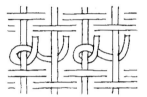

The Persian asymmetrical single knot.

Although the cooperatives produce only pile-weave carpets for the export market, village women also make flatweave kilims for their own use. Kilim is a plain-weave, weft-faced, slit-tapestry technique. The characteristic small slits are the result of discontinuous wefts that block in areas of solid color rather than continue from edge to edge across the width of the rug. The tightly packed wefts completely hide the warp.

The weaver starts her carpet with a few inches of flatweave. Typically in red and blue stripes, the kilim section stengthens the ends of the carpet and prevents the pile from unraveling when the finished rug is cut off the loom.

Now the design of the carpet begins to take shape, built up from row after row of colored knots. After each row of knots, two rows of plain weave anchor the knots in place, all packed tightly together using a beater *(kırkıt)* that resembles a comb. These tools are handcarved by village men from a hard wood such

38. The carpet starts with a few inches of flatweave.
(Photo David Jacobson)

39. Cennet Deneri tying knots.
40. After each row of knots, Sefaye Gül compacts the
pile using a beater. (Photo Dong Lin)

as oak. Some weavers now use durable metal beaters purchased in local shops. Next, special scissors shear the row of knots to a level pile, then the process is repeated — one row of knots, two rows of weft.

When tying a row of knots, the weaver works with one color at a time. She starts with the black knots that outline the motifs, then fills in all the red knots, then the blue knots, and so on. As the weaving progresses, she rolls the finished sections out of sight onto the lower warp beam. When repeating her pattern, the weaver cannot refer to the finished section of the carpet, and must therefore memorize her design as she works so that the top half is a symmetrical repeat of the bottom half.

For many daily tasks, villagers share the work, a custom called *imece*. Thus, women like to weave in pairs — mother and daughter, older sister and younger sibling, aunt and niece — the experienced weaver teaching and guiding her pupil. When woven as a dowry piece, the carpet will serve as a constant reminder in later years of the beloved family members who shared the young girl's work and put themselves into her carpet.

Socializing at the loom helps pass the time and alleviate boredom, and the work goes quickly. Depending on the width of the carpet, anywhere from two to five women can sit side by side at the loom. This accounts for the slight differences in color and design between the left and right side in some of the large carpets.

Although women often weave in groups on a single carpet, they do not share its profits. Typically, one woman provides the raw materials and the loom, decides on the design, and solicits others to help her on a trade or credit basis. When a weaver helps another and ties a certain number of knots, she is then owed the same number of knots when weaving her own rug. Every woman working on a communal carpet does, however, weave her own initials into the design.

After the completed carpet is cut from the loom, women braid the three-inch-long end threads into a fringe. The unused part of the warp still attached to the loom is removed and recycled. Women splice the short lengths of leftover warp threads into a continuous yarn and wind it into a ball ready for another warp.

The carpet is washed with cold water before delivery to the cooperative depot where the individual

41. After each rown of knots,
    Cennet Deneri uses special
    scissors to level the pile.

42. Tools of the trade: Handcarved
    wooden beater, scissors for clipping
    the knots, and drop spindles.

43. Ayşe Savran working indoors. Sarıahmetli 1995.

knots in every carpet must be tallied. To discourage loose and sloppy workmanship, weavers are paid by knot count rather than by the size of the carpet. Down on their hands and knees, women count the number of knots per row, multiplying by the number of warp threads. A carpet's value depends on the density of knots per square inch and the cooperatives maintain high standards of craftmanship, rejecting carpets that fail to meet their requirements. A woman who consistently produces poor work runs the risk of losing her family membership in the cooperative.

Weavers take pride in their competence at knotting and judge one another's work by technical mastery, defining a good carpet as one that is finely executed. A sixteen-square-foot carpet can have between 40,000 and 100,000 knots depending on the skills of the weaver. One Ayvacık weaver, Emine Hanım, once delivered a seventy-five-square-foot carpet boasting 740,000 knots (Powell 1987).

Working eight hours a day, a weaver can average around 5,000 knots, yet rarely can she complete a 100,000-knot carpet in twenty consecutive days because her time at the loom must be integrated into her household schedule. Daily chores cannot be postponed. Bread must be baked, the house kept clean, animals milked, yogurt and cheese prepared,

and water brought from the well. Women help their husbands with seasonal work in the fields, planting and harvesting crops, and find winter the best time for weaving. Most cooperative weavers manage to produce between three and five carpets a year.

Increasingly, weavers have had to enlarge the scale of their work to satisfy foreign customers requesting carpets for dining or living rooms. In 1989, members of the Sezgin family in Süleymanköy produced a 270-square-foot carpet commissioned by the British Museum in London for its Islamic Gallery — the only contemporary Oriental rug in the collection. The size of the carpet presented a challenge. The weavers had to build a special loom outdoors, and process the wool from two hundred sheep. In 1992, Ayvacık weavers produced their largest carpet ever for All Soul's College at Oxford University; it measures 380 square feet and contains approximately 3.5 million knots.

A weaver spends hours, weeks, months painstakingly tying knots. Moreover, she invests her time and energy in the very birth of the carpet — handling the fleece, carding fibers, spinning yarn, dyeing skeins, warping the loom. This personal imprint, this closeness of maker to materials, makes a village carpet special. The human hand has guided and controlled the raw materials and fashioned a thing of beauty. Our understanding of the manual processes of carpet making, the skills and expertise involved, the cost in time and labor, and the intimate relationship between artist and medium, increases our appreciation of the handmade object.

44a. Aysel Dönmez and Zahide Celebi braid the fringe. Ayvacık depot 1995.
44b. Typical braided fringe.

45. Dudu Öztoprak splices leftover warp yarn into new thread. Dudu is a well-traveled DOBAG weaver, having visited Japan, Norway, and Ireland to give public demonstrations of carpet weaving. Süleymanköy 1995.

46. Nazire Dönmez counts knots. Weavers deliver carpets to the DOBAG depot on Fridays when they are in town for the weekly market. Ayvacık 1995.

29

47. Members of the Sezgin family display the carpet commissioned by the British Museum. Süleymanköy 1989. (Photo Harald Böhmer)

AESTHETICS

Enter any village mosque in Turkey and carpet history literally lies before you. Pattern overlapping pattern, carpets of all ages cover the entire floor, layered by generations of village weavers. Many are prayer rugs, with the typical *mihrap* or niche design, and belong comfortably in a house of worship; others were woven for different purposes — as part of a young girl's dowry or for home furnishings and later donated to the mosque as a votive or pious offering, a custom known as *vakıf*. This type of gift can mark an auspicious occasion or a rite of passage — to celebrate a birth or marriage, or in memory of a deceased family member. Some rugs are given in lieu of fees when children attend Koran classes (Acar 1988:16-18).

48. Village mosque. Yuntdağ region 1981.
   (Photo Harald Böhmer)
49. The interior of Sarıahmetli mosque 1995.

These customs have preserved a chronology of traditional village designs for posterity. Much like a museum, the village mosque is a repository for a collection of carpets that informs us about regional variations and provides a record of change in colors, patterns, and motifs through time. Within this storehouse we find naturally dyed antique carpets over 100 years old alongside transitional hybrids made from a combination of vegetable and synthetic dyes and recent additions woven entirely with aniline-dyed wools. As historical documents, these carpets provide a rich source for studying the antecedents of contemporary village rugs.

Carpets woven by village women today belong to a folk tradition of carpet weaving that spread throughout Anatolia with successive migrations of nomadic tribes and settlers. We cannot accurately establish the precise origin of the designs, though some of the motifs (the octagon and the eight-point star, for example) have prototypes that can be traced to a pre-Islamic Central Asian source as well as to later waves of people who have been moving west-ward into Anatolia since the eleventh century — the Oğuz clans, the Turkmen tribes, and the nomadic Yörük groups. Modern carpet designs draw on this legacy of population shifts, cultural influences, and the development of local types.

Establishing origins based primarily on motifs is problematic because the ancient Near East was never a region of isolated, mutually exclusive cultures but rather a hotbed of intellectual and artistic borrowing. Since prehistoric times, Anatolia has been at the crossroads of cultures — a land bridge for mass movements of peoples from east and west, a pathway for armies on the march, and a well-traveled trade route between Europe and Asia. This continuous intercultural exchange brought fresh ideas and external influences into the realm of weavers both settled and nomadic. The traditional repertoire absorbed new motifs and design elements — a process that continues to this day. Village weavers have proved innovative and versatile in incorporating new themes into their rug patterns over the past decade.

Through the centuries, traditional Turkish carpet designs have managed to weather the storms of successive social upheavels and survive relatively intact by accommodating change. Tradition, by definition, is continuity; yet to remain relevant from one generation to the next as living, dynamic forms of expression, folk art must adapt to new situations and reflect the new life exiences of its makers. As people's ideas change, so do their artifacts. Conceptually, tradition is a reinterpretation of the past rather than a clone, and modern village carpets are rooted in contemporary community life, a product of their own time and place. They are old designs rethought and reinvented in new contexts.

Anatolian village carpets, in true folk-art fashion, have absorbed outside influences into their own vernacular without compromising their regional identity and design integrity. For example, the tulip and carnation motifs, intruders in the folk idiom, became geometric, stylized adaptations of the realistic floral motifs of the classical Ottoman court style. Considering the scope of artistic influences from diverse sources present throughout ancient Anatolia, it is remarkable that most of the traditional designs have endured with only minor alterations. Stability rather than change is the common principle: There are more similarities than differences between today's village carpets and those of six hundred years ago that are on exhibit in Istanbul's museums.

The design of each village carpet is determined by the cultural aesthetic, regional variants, and the weaver's own creativity. The cultural aesthetic defines the rules of composition; it is the grammar of a visual language shared by all village carpets, the structure upon which the design is built. It determines how the parts are organized into a whole, and how they relate to one another — a system of connections much like words in a sentence. Thus, the weaver works within a communal framework that sets stylistic boundaries and distinguishes her designs from those of other Oriental carpets. Carpets made by the DOBAG cooperative are easily recognizable as Turkish.

Limiting design choices to conform to a cultural formula is not a conscious thought process. Surrounded by traditional carpets all her life, the weaver knows intuitively what feels right in her ordered, visual world. As Cammann observes (1972:21), the design repertoire is absorbed on a daily basis: "It helps to recall that a single rug often served as the only form of decoration in a house or tent, and that the village mosque was often strictly plain except for the rugs scattered on its floor. Thus, rugs were usually the only things people had to look at. In the absence of any other furniture, they sat on them, ate upon them, visited on them, and slept on them: so, consciously or not, their eyes were constantly being attracted to study the patterns."

Whereas society is made of people, culture is made of ideas. Patterns of thought, or worldview, become patterns in the material expressions of a culture — its artifacts. The cultural aesthetic, then, is a cognitive model of the collective psyche that guides the individual's ability to compose — the internal made external. This mental template ties all village rugs into a single system of thought, manifested in the designs.

In village carpets, the cultural preference favors a geometric repertoire — straight lines rather than curves, stylized forms rather than organic, abstract shapes rather than pictorial representations, predictable rather than spontaneous arrangements. It is a controlling, restricted system of patterning compared with the multiple possibilities of freeform configurations.

The overall design is bilaterally symmetrical on a vertical axis — the left half a mirror image of the right, with a central field surrounded by a main border (*kesme su*) flanked by two smaller guard stripes (*ince su*). (For structural analysis and diagrams, see Glassie 1993:582.)

Stylistic concerns are also governed by the restraints of the medium. Geometry results from the weaving technique itself; warp and weft run at right angles to each other, favoring design elements with vertical, horizontal, and diagonal straight lines rather than curvilinear shapes. Moreover, the pile-weaving technique produces a squarish knot further accentuated by the use of thick woollen yarn. The knot, as minimal unit, builds the motif much like the pointillist technique of Impressionism created images from colored dots. Therefore, its a question of scale; the smaller the unit, the finer the detail. A delicate yarn such as silk can produce a carpet with hundreds of knots per square inch — a suitable medium for the minutely detailed, naturalistic motifs of the Ottoman court aesthetic.

When weaving geometric designs, the weaver can easily repeat a motif by counting the knots. A mathematical formula helps her memorize and duplicate the patterns, especially when the finished part of the carpet is rolled out of sight on the cloth beam.

The predisposition to nonpictorial designs in Turkish village carpets is often attributed to Muslim taboos against depicting human and animal images lest it lead to idolatry (Cammann 1972:11). However, some motifs were acquired from non-Islamic cultures along the trade routes, and a well-established geometric inventory existed long before the introduction of Koranic proscriptions. Possibly, Islam's proscriptions merely reinforced the artistic bias for geometric shapes (Acar 1982:38).

Following cultural paradigms of composition, the weaver chooses designs that fit into a social context — traditional designs handed down within her family or community, patterns that denote regional identity and proclaim village affiliation. As dialects within the language of the cultural aesthetic, regional designs can be specific to a village or communal within a district.

50. Carpet woven by Cennet Yılmaz. Villagers call this design *vazo selvi*, cypress vase. Örselli 1992.

51. Carpet woven by Şerife Uğur, which she simply calls *yeni desen*, new design. Sarıahmetli 1992.

52. *Çarklı* design.

53. *Oklu* design.

54. *Yıldız,* star.

Carpets are often classified by the names of their marketplaces, such as Ezine, Kula, Bergama. Within each locality, weavers themselves categorize their designs, naming them after the large primary motifs (octagons, rhomboids, eight-pointed stars, and so on) in the central field — *beş tabak* (five plates), *oklu* (with arrows), *çarklı* (with wheels). Similarly, in the United States, quiltmakers give names to the geometric patterns they sew — Drunkard's Path, Grandmother's Basket, Flock of Geese.

Art historians and rug scholars also have a shared vocabulary of carpet names from a different source — works by the Old Masters. Artists such as Hans Holbein and Lorenzo Lotto often included Turkish carpets with distinctive motifs in their paintings. These designs took the names of those artists. For example, the fifteenth-century Flemish painter Hans Memling pictured rugs with octagonal motifs in his paintings and this design is now known as the Memling Gül (the octagonal *gül* was once a Turkmen tribal emblem). However, village weavers do not use these terms to describe their patterns; they are typologies imposed from outside the folk culture, an academic nomenclature to identify carpets for study purposes. Even urban dealers have been known to invent fanciful names, pandering to the buyers' notions of the exotic Orient.

Memling gül.

Unfortunately, we lack standardization in design labels and classifications; weavers might use one name, art historians another. The so-called wine cup border is a case in point. According to Walter Denny, "the design was not intended to represent a wine cup, and the weaver had never seen a wine cup" (1973:9). Village women call this design leaf border.

Wine cup border design.

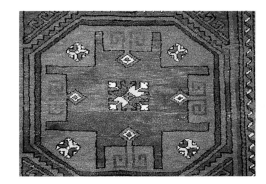

55. Three interpretations of the *elekli* design, named after the shape inside the octogon, which resembles a village sieve, or *elek*.

The cooperatives do not select the designs or supply cartoons on graph paper as a guide for the weaver. She has memorized a selection of village prototypes, passed on from mother to daughter, and interpets them in her own way. She improvises, refashions, and updates tradition, developing her own style. Each design is unique — an idiosyncratic variation on a theme rather than an imitation of another carpet.

Like the storyteller whose favorite folk tale is never the same story twice told but a reworked version of the original, the weaver never repeats the same design identically. Each recounting of the tale, each reinterpretation of the pattern, will be a new creation, not a mechanical reproduction. Likewise,

two weavers following the same design formula will produce two different carpets. The artisan is inventor as well as technician, and this sets the handmade carpet apart from the machine-made rug with its capacity for infinite copies. With their seemingly endless permutations of shapes and colors within basic formats, village rugs exemplify diversity.

The third element in design composition centers on individual creativity, for carpet making is the main artistic vehicle of village women. The constraints of the cultural aesthetic and regional types still allow for self-expression in the small scatter motifs inserted in spaces between the large, primary motifs. The fill-in motifs, called *sinekli*, "with flies," are ornamental details, randomly placed; they can be removed without disturbing the foundation of the design. They are also interchangeable in that many alternative modules can fill the same slot and function equivalently. This gives the weaver the opportunity to make personal choices from her own catalog of favorite motifs.

35

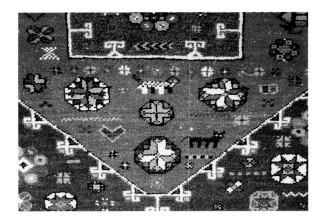

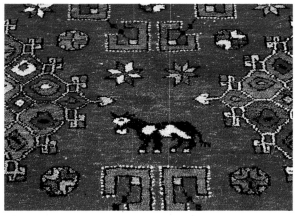

56. Whimsical figures fill the spaces between the primary motifs.

Through the scatter motifs, we get a sense of the weaver's presence and, as the minimal unit of composition, each small motif is not unlike the weaver's position in society — a symbolic equivalent or allomotif. Both fit into a village or community framework, which in turn fits into the broader cultural system. Both share a common relationship as the least common denominator in a structural hierarchy.

We find evidence of women using their carpets as a medium for self-expression in what I call the whimsy phenomenon. It started in the mid-1980s; one weaver, somewhere in the Yuntdağ region, began to substitute for her geometric scatter motifs small pictorial figures — a cat, a house, a vase of flowers, sheep, ducks, butterflies, and other recognizable shapes. She started a trend, and others followed suit. Soon the carpets teemed with whimsical figures. The idea proliferated and spread to the Ayvacık cooperative, and the whimsical figure has become very much a part of the regional style.

The change in the repertoire of random motifs reflects a change in the weaver's attitude to her work. With obvious self-confidence, women now take artistic risks, playing with their designs in imaginative and innovative ways. The carpets Cennet Deneri wove during her visits to San Francisco's natural history museum incorporate motifs that document her recent experiences — a Lufthansa airplane, a yellow school bus, fish from the museum's Aquarium — alongside her village house and her two children. In 1994 Cennet positioned her loom under a suspended whale skeleton in the museum; she wove this image into her carpet — possibly the first whale skeleton ever to appear in a Turkish carpet!

Cennet Deneri's carpets visually record events in her life, even though they are woven for sale, not for herself. Some say that when folk art goes commercial — made predominantly for outsiders — it loses its vitality and originality, and artists become mass-producing robots. If weavers just wanted to sell carpets, they would probably stick to the simple, geometric shapes they know so well. For Cennet, and others like her, weaving carpets gives them pleasure. Playfulness in the designs suggests creative growth, not mechanical reproduction.

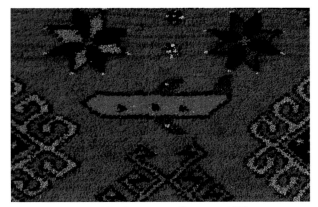

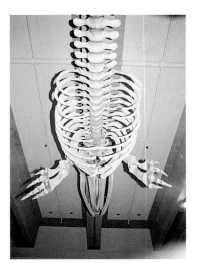

57. A Lufthansa motif in Cennet Deneri's carpet. 1992.

58. Whale skeleton suspended above Cennnet's loom.
    California Academy of Sciences 1994.

In the 1990s, experimentation went a step further.
When weavers first introduced pictorial motifs into
their repertoire, all the figures appeared the same way
up consistently throughout the carpet, making it easy
to recognize the top and bottom of the carpet, as
woven, from the vertical direction of the figures. In
1994, Şerife Uğur, from the village of Sarıahmetli,
wove a row of quails at the beginning of her carpet,
and repeated the motifs upside down at the end of her
carpet, making the top half a perfect mirror image
of the bottom half (see catalog of carpet designs,
no. 27). Before this, whimsical motifs were only
randomly placed, not thoughtfully arranged to
balance. In 1995 I noticed a similar treatment on a
carpet in Örselli. Two blue birds facing each other in
the bottom half of a carpet were inverted in the top
half. Although pictorial motifs still function as fill-in
embellishments floating in space, some weavers have
chosen deliberately to anchor them as structural
elements in the composition.

Women continue to explore design possibilities.
In 1995, two carpets newly arrived at the DOBAG
gallery in San Francisco grabbed my attention as
being different from the rest of the shipment from the
Yuntdağ cooperative. Both carpets were woven by
twenty-two-year-old Saadet Yılmaz from the village
of Örselli. They looked like samplers. Saadet had
assembled every motif in the Yuntdağ repertoire —
border motifs, major design motifs, and traditional
geometric fill-in shapes — and placed them throughout the main field. Usually border motifs remain in

59. Whale motif incorporated in carpet (on the right).

37

the borders, and the large primary shapes are not
reduced to the size of random motifs. Additionally,
Saadet had woven her first name in full rather than
use her initials.

In the Yuntdağ cooperative, weavers are finding
new ways to interpret old ideas in the striped, kilim
end borders *(baş örgüsü)* of their carpets. Antique
carpets from this region often have highly decorative
kilim sections. When weavers worked for dealers, for
low pay, the kilim ends were less ornate, with plain
red and blue stripes to cut down on time. Today
Yuntdağ weavers are once again using a variety of
colors in their end borders, and adding rows of small
pile tufts. Whereas Yuntdağ weavers use the tufts
decoratively, in the Ayvacık region a single pile
button is used to identify village of origin (Eiland III
1995). Each weaver puts her own village emblem in
the center of the kilim section, in the same way that

60. Saadet Yılmaz weaves her name into her carpet. 1995.

61. Decorative kilim sections on Yuntdağ carpets.

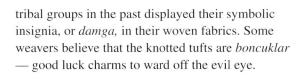

62. Yuntdağ decorative pile buttons.

63. Ayvacık village emblem woven in the kilim end.

64. Çamkalabak weaver. 1992.

tribal groups in the past displayed their symbolic insignia, or *damga,* in their woven fabrics. Some weavers believe that the knotted tufts are *boncuklar* — good luck charms to ward off the evil eye.

Motifs fill every available space in a carpet's main field, leaving no areas of plain color where the eye can rest. This characteristic can be found in other forms of Islamic art, a stylistic trait often referred to as *horror vacui,* or aversion to empty space. The clothing of village women shows the same preference for patterns bustling with shapes and color. For their traditional baggy pants *(şalvar),* blouses, and headscarves, they choose all-over patterned fabrics that, to Western eyes, lack a sense of color coordination. Seated at her loom, the village weaver and her carpet present a doubly colorful sight!

To personalize her carpet further, a weaver works her initials into the design, usually at the top of the carpet, often adding the date and the initial of her village as well. She also makes her own color choices, for there are no aesthetic rules assigning specific colors to certain motifs although all Anatolian rugs show a preference for red and blue.

The weaver possesses a vocabulary of names for the traditional geometric motifs she uses, drawn from familiar objects in her surroundings — apple, blossom, camel's foot, oak leaf, ram's horn, comb. (For further information on motifs from everyday life, see Paquin 1983.) The same motif may have a different name from weaver to weaver and from village to village. Many of the motifs did not originate in the villages of western Turkey. These basic shapes have a long history and can be found in Selçuk carpets from the thirteenth century as well as

65. Most women weave their initials and a date into their carpets.

66. Motifs are outlined in black or other colors to emphasize the shape and to form a transition where two colors meet.

67. *Elibelinde* variant in an eighteenth century Yörük carpet. Vakıflar Museum, Istanbul.

68. *Elibelinde* motif in a DOBAG carpet. 1994.

69. Yuntdağ carpets are distinguished by the *elibelinde* motif at the beginning and end of the carpet. Villagers call the motif "arm's akimbo."

carpets from other countries. Though motifs may stay the same visually, their meanings, however, can change through time. For instance, variations of the octagon appear in folk art throughout the world. To the Turkmen, the octagonal *gül* was an emblem of tribal identity, a meaning that cannot have the same social or personal significance for those outside the group or to people living today.

Similarly, in the carpet literature, the goddess of Anatolia motif, the *elibelinde,* may be traced back to around 6000 B.C. (Opie 1993:241), to a time when female deities reigned over the lives of agricultural people. Some historians assume that any motif resembling the *elibelinde* since that time represents the goddess. Village weavers call the shape "arms akimbo." Murray Eiland comments that "the coming of the Indo-Europeans was the beginning of the end for goddess-dominated religions. . . . So when we find figures remotely suggestive of female forms in Anatolian kilims, be they from the nineteenth century or the fifteenth century, any resemblence to goddess figures could hardly have been intended by the weavers. Such forms, even if at some dim time in the past they may have related to religious beliefs including goddesses, must surely have lost all significance to the Anatolian peasantry over the last four thousand years" (1990:39). Thus, without supporting evidence or knowledge of the symbolic system of the folk cultures using the motif, diachronic interpretations of symbolic content in motifs must be speculative.

Symbols function as a visual form of communication only between people who share the same symbolic language. Symbolism is embedded in a group's belief system, to be analyzed synchronically in its own sociocultural context, its own time and place. A symbol may convey religious, totemic, magical, or talismanic messages to those who understand the visual vocabulary. A tribal motif incorporated into a household textile or an item of clothing as an amulet to ward off the evil eye does not serve this protective function when used in societies without this superstitious belief.

As cultures vary in their beliefs, so do the symbolic ideas invested in their folk art. In one culture, red may connote happiness (positive); in another, it may signify danger (negative). The swastika is an ancient motif found throughout the world on pottery, tiles, textiles, baskets, and other art forms, including Pomo Indian baskets and Navajo Indian blankets. To most people today it stands for the racism of the Hitler regime in Germany. Likewise, symbols of an Islamic culture may embody beliefs that cannot be translated across religious boundaries. (For an unusual interpretation of Islamic symbolism, see Cammann 1972.) Thus, the same shape can evoke multiple emotions and associations in different people from different backgrounds.

Along the silk route from China to Anatolia, carpet weavers borrowed motifs from one another. Some Turkish village carpets feature design elements also found in contemporary carpets from Kazakstan. Chinese cloudbands appear in Persian carpets and as a main border motif in antique and modern Yuntdağ carpets. Weavers call the motif *koç boynuzu,* or ram's horn.

However, appropriating a motif does not mean accepting the beliefs associated with it. Discussing Oriental carpets in general, Jan David Winitz writes: "As the twentieth century progressed, the meaning behind the patterns became so obscured that, in some cases, weavers began knotting carpets consisting entirely of patterns from other groups. When we view a rug woven by the Baluche people of Afghanistan which reproduces the ancient motifs of the Caucasus Mountains 1,500 miles away, we may safely assume that any symbolic significance has been lost" (1985:1).

The attribution of symbolic or mystical content to motifs in contemporary village carpets according to the meanings of those motifs in the distant past or from other cultures is, therefore, academically unsound. The people who make and use the carpets — those who assign the symbolic meanings — are best equipped to provide interpretation. Unfortunately, carpet weavers of the past, long since dead and gone, cannot tell us how they felt about their visual world. Anonymous, unlettered, ordinary folk, they left no written records of their lives, nothing to reveal the depths of their imagery, only the mute artifact to be deciphered. "Ottoman literature has almost no tradition of writing about the industrial classes. . . . Few wrote about them, and they didn't write about themselves" (Quartaert 1986:25). Therefore, we can never be sure what a carpet motif of the past meant to the people who used it and, without empirical data, imposing symbolic meaning is merely theoretical exercise.

The art historian is skilled at tracing, through documents and other secondary sources, the origins of designs and their diffusion routes. The ethnographer seeks answers in the present, focusing on living artists — people who still make carpets. Ethnographic methodology has the interpretive advantage of working with informants who can unlock the symbolic code and provide reliable information to substantiate scholarly hypothesis. As a primary source of information, today's village weavers can tell us the significance, if any, of their designs. Yet, informants are not always a foolproof source; they may give the sort of information they think the interviewer wants, in an attempt to please. Although the historical and ethnographic approaches are different, they can both contribute to our understanding of Oriental carpets.

Moreover, we must guard against reading latent meaning where none was intended. Much like a Rorschach ink blot, image associations often tell us more about the mind of the person doing the interpretation than about his or her subject. We cannot assume that all carpet motifs are loaded with potent messages ripe for translation. It is possible that the weaver simply liked a particular shape and chose it for decorative reasons — art for art's sake. "Those among the symbolists who see complex theological and philosophical systems in the designs are perhaps reading too much into the work of simple, straightforward people" (Landreau and Yohe 1983:70). When asked, weavers in the DOBAG cooperatives will tell you the names of their carpet designs and the motifs, but rarely offer symbolic interpretations. Meanings have either been lost over time or weavers choose not to share them with outsiders. Yusuf Durul cites a standard response among weavers: "When Yörük women are asked about the meaning of these motifs, they usually reply: They were handed down to us from our family. They bring us luck" 1977:63).

The two cooperatives cater to the export market, yet foreign consumer tastes have had no influence on village designs or the traditional palette. Weavers can remain true to their own aesthetic and still satisfy overseas customers because the world market is diverse. American, Asian, and European tastes in carpets differ. One country prefers medallion carpets in dark colors; another prefers overall patterns in lighter shades. What sells in Tokyo might not sell in Oslo.

Nevertheless, international trade has influenced production in one aspect — the size of the carpet. In their own homes, villagers cover the entire floor with numerous overlapping rugs of a size that is easily portable — a vestige of the nomadic lifestyle of the past. Small rugs can be rolled up and carried for easy transportation to dealers in city bazaars or for selling at weekly markets; when cleaning house, small rugs can be taken outdoors and given a shake to remove the dirt. (I have yet to see a vacuum cleaner in a village house.) Even when villagers go on a summer picnic to the river or other scenic spot, they take along their carpets to sit on.

According to Uğur Ayyıldız (1982:16), rug sizes have names in Turkey. Standard dimensions include: *çeyrek,* 135 cm x 90 cm (4 1/2 ft. x 3 ft.) *karyola, 220 c*m x 150 cm (7 1/4 ft. x 5 ft.) *kelle*, 300 cm x 200 cm (10 ft. x 6 1/2 ft.) *taban*, rugs over 6 square meters (64 sq. ft.)

To meet the demand for large carpets in Western homes, villagers built bigger looms to produce eight- by twelve-foot carpets, and weavers learned to adapt their designs. Large carpets tested the weavers' design competence. How do you enlarge the design without compromising stylistic laws?

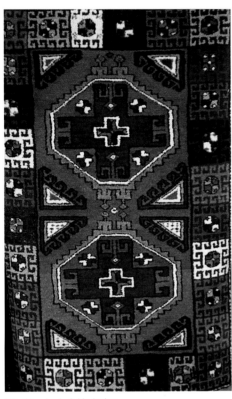

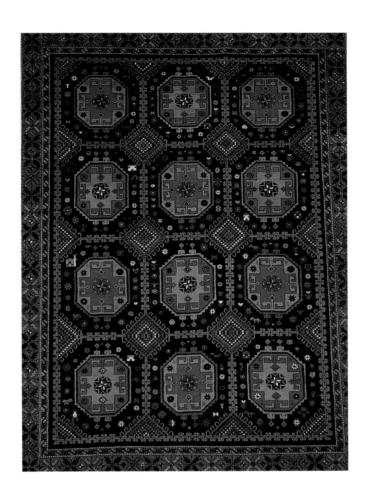

70. Standard *elekli* design.
71. *Elekli* motif repeated in large carpet.

Weavers solved the problem by repeating the large motifs rather than by blowing up elements of the design. They chose not to alter the scale of the motifs and their structural relationships, but to simply extend the original borders outward and duplicate the design to fill the space. Imagine four carpets laid edge to edge with the adjacent borders removed. Thus, in a design with a central medallion, the motif stays the same size and becomes a repetitive element. The visual effect is similar to that of the patterning of the mosque floor or villagers' homes, with their many overlapping rugs. Through repetition, weavers maintain a design balance that feels right and fits the cultural rules governing composition.

To summarize, today's village carpets, like other folk-art genres, act as a connecting thread between the weaver and her cultural, regional, and personal identity. As a shared aesthetic, the designs denote her Turkish heritage. They connect past and present — a link in time. Regional variants connect the weaver to her family and community — a link to place. The small motifs provide a medium for personal expression and satisfy individual creativity — a link to her inner self. Within the stylistic boundaries defined by tradition the weaver improvises, experiments, and expands her repertoire in new directions. This, too, is part of the tradition. Village carpets represent a living tradition of Anatolian carpet making with a long history of incorporating change.

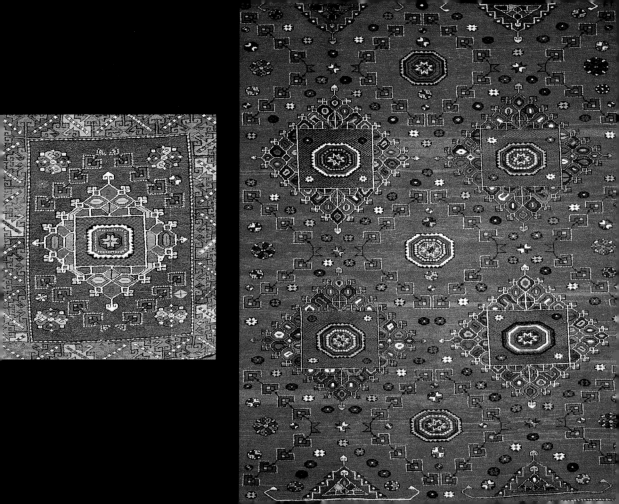

The carpet designs described in this catalog represent the repertoire of weavers in the Ayvacık and Yuntdağ cooperatives. Most designs continue to be regional to this day: Weavers in the Ayvacık cooperative stick to their own village designs, as do weavers from the Yuntdağ region further south. Many of the geometric motifs have antecedents in the Turkmen *güls* or tribal emblems originating in Central Asia. (For a catalog of the major and secondary *güls*, see the diagrams in Ford 1981:177.) The Vakıflar Museum and the Museum of Turkish and Islamic Art *(Türk ve İslam Eserleri Müzesi)* in Istanbul both house major carpet collections including thirteenth-century carpets from the Selçuk dynasty that have motifs and designs similar to those of modern village carpets. It is amazing that these designs have been handed down from mother to daughter with only minor variations for over seven hundred years.

The names cited for each design are the terms used by village weavers to describe their carpets. Often the name of a design can vary from village to village.

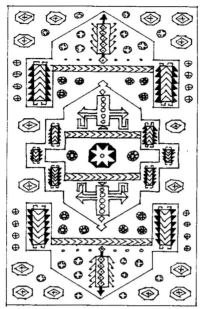

1. AKBAŞ

Weaver: Müşerref Sezgin
Village: Süleymanköy
Date: 1993
At the top of this design (mirrored at the bottom) is a triangular shape with two rectangles hanging down at each side, above the central medallion. This shape is similar to the bride's headdress, from which this design — *akbaş* or white head — takes its name. When this section is yellow, it is called *sarıbaş*, or yellow head. Some villagers call it *büyük bas*, big head. An eighteenth-century Ezine carpet with this design is on exhibit at the Museum of Turkish and Islamic Art.

2. TURNALİ

Weaver: Neslihan Öter
Village: Çamkalabak
Date: 1995
Villagers call this pattern *turnalı*, with cranes, after the diagonal chevrons resembling birds in flight. Some rug scholars interpret the central lozenge medallion as the multipetaled lotus flower, from the lotus seat of Buddha. The Metropolitan Museum of Art in New York and the Vakıflar Warehouse in Ankara each has an eighteenth-century version of this design from Çanakkale. The motif can also be found in a fifteenth-century painting by Domenico Ghirlandaio in the Uffizi, Florence.

2B. Lozenge medallion from a nineteenth-century Makri rug (Eiland 1990:50).

45

72. Standard *turnalı* design in small carpet.
73. *Turnalı* motif repeated on a large scale.

3. OKLU

Weaver: Semiha Yılmaz
Village: Karagömlek
Date: 1989

Oklu means with arrows. Carpets with this dominant motif are also known as Ezine after the village of that name. Harald Böhmer observed that "the similarity between the *oklu* motif and the Tekke *gül* derives from the fact that the Tekke Turkmen of the steppes east of the Caspian Sea and the Yörük nomads in Anatolia are of similar descent. It is a cosmic diagram of the four cardinal points already found on the backs of Chinese mirrors of the Han dynasty (206 B.C.-220 A.D.)" (1983:360). Some villagers call this design *kızıllı* (from the old word for red) after the traditional red field. Henry Glassie cites other village names for this design, including *çakmak,* or pocket lighter, *kumburun* from the village of that name, and *kara börek — kara* means black, and *börek* is a flaky pastry (1993:614-15).

In the Yörük village of Çamkalabak this design has special significance. An *oklu* carpet covers the saddle of the bride's horse during the wedding procession to her new home (Atlıhan 1993:81-85). An eighteenth-century *oklu* carpet from Konya is in the Vakıflar Museum. In 1988 the British Museum in London chose this design when it commissioned a 270-square-foot carpet DOBAG carpet for its Islamic Art Gallery.

46

3B. A variant of the *oklu* design from the Yuntdağ region.

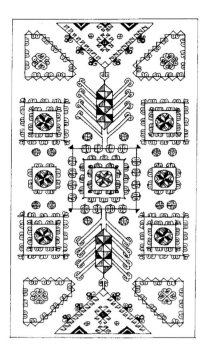

4. ALTIN TABAK

Weaver: Sefaye Erdoğan
Village: Süleymanköy
Date: 1995

Altın tabak, or golden plate, takes its name from the decorative gold edging on the square shapes. In Çamkalabak there is a variant called *beş tabak,* five plates, and a carpet with this design must be included in every girl's dowry (Atlıhan 1983:80). Erdman refers to this design as a Holbein Type IV (1977:35).

5. YÖRÜK
Weaver: Emine Çalımlı
Village: Çınarpınar
Date: 1993
Some Ayvacık weavers call this design *yörük* after the tribal nomads. In Çamkalabak it is known as *yeşil bacak*, green legs; other villages call it *kozaklı*, possibly after the Kozak district in the Manisa area.

6. YENGEÇLI
Weaver: Gülseren Kuş
Village: Keçikaya
Date: 1993
Yengeçli, meaning with crab after the overall shape of the design, is also called *çengelli,* with hooks, after the many small latchhooks in the design. McMullen calls it a garden pattern Bergama type (1972, pl. no. 11). A nineteenth-century Bergama carpet with this design is in the Metropolitan Museum of Art, New York.

7. KOZAK
Weaver: Kadriye Şen
Village: Pınardere
Date: 1993
Kozak is a region of sixteen villages north of Bergama.

47

8. LAMBALI

Weaver: Gülseren Kuş
Village: Keçikaya
Date: 1994

Ayvacik villagers call this design *lambalı,* with lamps. The triangular motifs resemble the hanging lamps in village mosques. The tree-of-life motif, *hayat ağacı,* is above and below the central medallion.

9. SANDIKLI

Weaver: Cennet Uslu
Village: Örselli
Date: 1992

The square shapes are likened to the dowry or trousseau chest (*sandık,* box or compartment). Also called *büyük sandık,* big box, the squares are surrounded by *elma* motifs (apple, or apple blossoms). This design can be seen in a sixteenth-century carpet and an eighteenth-century Çanakkale rug on exhibit at the Museum of Turkish and Islamic Art, and in a nineteenth-century Yuntdağ carpet in the village mosque at Örencik.

10. ÇARKLI

Weaver: Gülşen Özkan
Village: Ayvacık
Date: 1995

Çarklı, with wheels, refers to the cogs of a machine wheel. In the Turkish Ministry of Culture carpet exhibit in Istanbul, the design is called *çarkıfelek,* wheel of fortune. Jon Thompson believes the Bergama wheel is derived from the Buddhist eight-petaled lotus symbol (1982:8-12). The Museum of Turkish and Islamic Art displays a fifteenth-century Bergama carpet with this motif, called Holbein Type III.

10B. Motif from a fifteenth-century western Anatolian carpet in the Museum of Turkish and Islamic Art.

11. HOLBAYN

Weaver: Emine Güler
Village: Süleymanköy
Date: 1995

The original village name for this design appears to have been lost, and weavers now use the same name as the art historians do, Holbein, written in Turkish as *holbayn*. It is the only design in the DOBAG repertoire that does not have a village term. The main motif — the endless knot or knotted band — can be seen in several paintings by the German artist Hans Holbein the Younger (1497-1543) and is called Holbein Type I. (For more information on Holbein rugs, see Yetkin 1981:43-72.) The contour knot can also be found in the center of the Kızıl Ayak *gül* from Turkestan (Ford 1981:177). The Museum of Turkish and Islamic Art has a Uşak example from the end of the fifteenth century as well as sixteenth-century examples from Konya and western Anatolian (Erdmann 1977:28-36). All Souls College at Oxford University chose the Holbein design when it commissioned a 380-square-foot carpet in 1992, the largest carpet ever made by DOBAG weavers, with 3.5 million knots.

The endless knot, according to the textile historian Diane Carroll, has a talismanic function. "Complex interlace patterns are almost universally believed to have protective powers, guarding against the evil eye. The tendency when looking at such a pattern is to trace the path of the interlace visually, thus keeping the eye moving. (It was the fixed stare that was considered dangerous.)" (1982:86).

12. ELEKLI

Weaver: Havva Kurt
Village: Çınarpınar
Date: 1994

The shape inside the octagon is called *elek,* (the name for a kitchen sieve) in the village of Çınarpınar. Ersu Pekın refers to the shape simply as *haç*, or cross (1988:109). The same design can be seen on a fourteenth-century fresco in Florence (Erdmann 1977:24).

12B. Lesghi medallion, Butterfield and Butterfield auction catalog, 16 September 1981, lot no. 183.

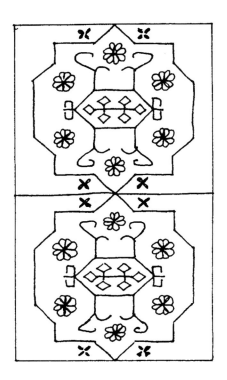

13. ÇİÇEK
Weaver: Ayşe Çevik
Village: Ereçek
Date: 1993
In the Ayvacık region this design is called *çiçek,* or flower blossom. Some young weavers call it "the letter Z" (the Roman alphabet replaced Arabic in 1928).

13B. Motif from a Shiraz rug, described as a "stylized crab" in the Sotheby Park Bernet auction catalog, 14 October 1978, lot no. 72.

13C. Border cartouche, which Schuyler Cammann (1972:16) terms "bird-like forms" derived from an ancient sunbird symbol, on a seventeenth-century, so-called Transylvania rug in the Victoria and Albert Museum, London.

13D. Border cartouche on a Chinese rug (no date), Butterfield and Butterfield auction catalog, 16 September 1981, lot no. 354.

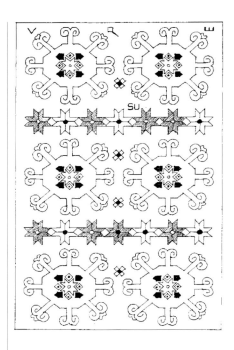

14. BURGU
Weaver: Şerife Uğur
Village: Sarıahmetli
Date: 1993
Burgu means corkscrew. Some weavers call this motif *burma tabak,* twisted plate.

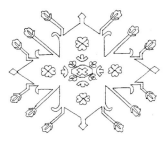

15B. Kazak carpet motif with radiating spokes, called the "palace design" (Lewis 1920:273).

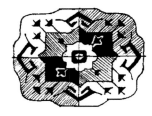

15C. *Tekke gül* motif from a nineteenth-century carpet, Butterfield and Butterfield auction catalog, 16 September 1981, lot no. 179.

15. BÜYÜK ÇIÇEK SANDIK ILE

Weaver: Şaziye Aktaş
Village: Sarıahmetli
Date: 1993

The name means large blossoms in compartments after the stemmed blossoms radiating from the central cross. Some weavers call the design *tabaklı*, with plates. Böhmer (1989:179-81) has dubbed it the Foschi carpet, having identified this motif in a 1540 painting by the Florentine master Pierfrancesco Foschi in the Galleria Corsini, Florence . Cathryn Cootner describes it as a *Tekke Güllü-gül* (1982:6). Pekın states that many rug dealers refer to this design as "eagle Kazak" (1988:150).

16. TÜRKMEN GÜLÜ
Weaver: Gönül Koç
Village: Misvak
Date: 1994

The motif is an ancient Turkman emblem, and Böhmer calls it the "Turk rosette" (1989:179). In the Yuntdağ, villagers call it *burma elma*, twisted apple, and in Ayvacık it is also known as *burma gül*, twisted rose. Opie refers to the rosette as a variant of the "knot of destiny" motif and connects it to the endless-knot motif "that appears in Chinese rugs and is one of the eight Buddhist symbols of good fortune" (1981:34). (For detailed analysis of this motif as *elibelinde*, or arm's akimbo, and its origin in the Chinese cosmic symbol *yün chien*, or cloud collar, from the Han dynasty, 206 B.C.-220 A.D., see Böhmer and Brüggemann 1983:60-78.)

In 1987 two DOBAG weavers wove a carpet with this design during their weaving demonstrations in Oslo, and later presented the finished rug to King Olaf of Norway. Since then, village weavers call this design "the King carpet."
The Museum of Turkish and Islamic Art has a thirteenth-century Selçuk carpet with this motif and an eighteenth-century example from western Anatolia.

17. KILIM DESENI
Weaver: Pakize Acarkoç
Village: Örselli
Date: 1994

To many weavers, this design reminds them of the typical hooked octagons on kilim rugs. Pekın identifies the motif as *karaburun*, black nose (1988:93); *karaburun* is also the name of a promontory and town in Izmir province where carpets are made. Historians use the term Memling Gül because the motif can be seen in fifteenth-century paintings by the Flemish artist Hans Memling. Erdmann gives a nineteenth-century example of the "hooked octagon" (1977:64-65, pl. no. 62). The same hooked motif can be found on the secondary *gül* of the Süleyman Turkmen (Ford 1981:177, *gül* no. 35). In Kazak carpets, the shape has been described as a "moghan medallion" (Butterfield and Butterfield auction catalog, 2 April 1981, lots no. 17, 394, 401, 404, 409).

18. CAMI

Weaver: Kadriye Çetin
Village: Karagömlek
Date: 1995

Weavers around Erecek call this overall pattern *cami*, or mosque. Böhmer writes that "the quartered lozenge-shaped motif in diagonally identical colors closely resembles the Dyrnak *güls* of certain Turkmen tribes living in the steppes east of the Caspian Sea" (1983:361).

18B. Dyrnak *gül* of the Yomut and Imrell Turkmen.

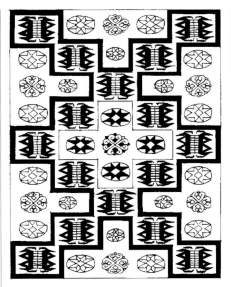

19. ŞEYTAN TIRNAĞI

Weaver: Ayşe Sönmez
Village: Örselli
Date: 1993

In the Yuntdağ, this design is called *şeytan tırnağı*, or devil's claw, after the hooked square shapes within the boxes. (See also Böhmer 1989:183-84.) Örençık mosque in Manisa has a nineteenth-century example, and the Museum of Turkish and Islamic Art displays a nineteenth-century version from Çanakkale. Ayvacık weavers call it *baratlı* after the name of a Yörük tribe, and the Turkish Ministry of Culture in Istanbul uses the same name.

20. EZINE TABAK

Weaver: Hanife Çetinkaya
Village: Karagömlek
Date: 1993

Ezine is a village in the Ayvacık area, and *tabak* means plate. The Turkish Ministry of Culture describes this design as "a repeating fertility symbol composed of four *koç boynuzu*, or ram's horn motifs, arranged in a checkerboard pattern." An eighteenth-century example from Çanakkale is in the Museum of Turkish and Islamic Art. Brüggeman sees this motif as a derivation of the Chinese *yün chien*, or cloud collar symbol (Böhmer and Brüggemann 1983:204).

53

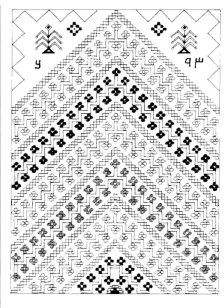

21. VAZO SELVI

Weaver: Cennet Yılmaz
Village: Örselli
Date: 1992

Villagers use the tern *vazo selvi,* cypress vase. Böhmer says "the central motif in the medallion has sprung from a vase" (1983:362). The overall design is categorized as a double-ended prayer rug *(seccade)* with a *mihrap,* or niche, top and bottom. Scholars call this type of medallion Transylvanian because seventeenth-century carpets with this design were found in churches in the Transylvania Alps of Romania, once part of the Hungarian Empire, though they were probably woven in the Bergama region. Böhmer compares the medallion to the *gül* of the Chaudor Turkmen from the steppes south of the Aral Sea (1989:182). The design can also be seen in European paintings of the seventeenth and eighteenth centuries. The Museum of Turkish and Islamic Art houses a seventeenth-century version.

22. ÜZÜM

Weaver: Gülistan Coşkun
Village: Sarıahmetli
Date: 1993

Weavers call this design *üzüm,* or grape. In some villages it is known as *cıngıl,* meaning a small bunch of grapes on a side shoot.

23. KÜÇÜK MIHRAP

Weaver: Fatma Can
Village: Erecek
Date: 1990

In the Ayvacık region, the name of this design means small *mihrap* or niche.

 54

24. BÜYÜK YILDIZ

Weaver: Cennet Deneri
Village: Örselli
Date: 1994

Büyük yıldız means big star. Art historians refer to this "winged medallion" as the Crivelli *gül* because the motif appears in paintings of the Annunciation by Carlo Crivelli in the Staedelsches Kunstinstitut, Frankfurt, and in the National Gallery, London, painted in 1482 and 1486 (Pinner 1993:245). Pinner finds similar motifs on Roman mosaics in Cirencester, England, from the third century A.D., and from Boxmoor, England, from the second century A.D.; he also links the shape to the inner motif of a Tekke Turkmen *gül* from the fifteenth century (Pinner 1993:245-52). The winged medallion can be seen on an eighteenth-century Anatolian rug at the Museum of Turkish and Islamic Art.

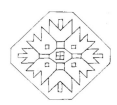

24B. Motif from a nineteenth-century Kazak rug, Sotheby Parke Bernet auction catalog, 20 January 1979, lot no. 33.

24C. Motif from a 1951 Kazakstan carpet in the private collection of Toby Lumpkin, Seattle.

24D. Border motif in an eighteenth-century Konya carpet, the Museum of Turkish and Islamic Art.

24E. The winged medallion appears in an Anatolian rug fragment from the fifteenth century in the Imparmüvészeti Muséum, Budapest.

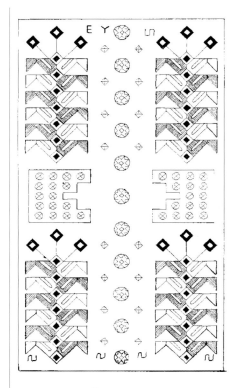

25. HAYAT AĞACI

Weaver: Emine Yalçın
Village: Karagömlek
Date: 1992

Hayat Ağacı is the "tree of life" design.

26. BAHÇELI
Weaver: Kadriye Keleş
Village: Pinardere
Date: 1996
Bahçeli means having a garden. Two tree-of-life motifs are on either side of the central lozenge.

27. YENI DESEN
Weaver: Şerife Uğar
Village: Sarıahmetli
Date: 1992
The weaver, Şerife Uğar, had no particular name for her design and simply called it *yeni* or new design, signifying that it was not a traditional design within her family. This type of garden design is common in the Yuntdağ district. An eighteenth-century Bergama version is in the Museum of Turkish and Islamic Art. Şerife has added a personal touch — a row of small birds at the beginning and end of her carpet.

BORDER DESIGNS

Typically, each carpet has a main border flanked by two smaller guard borders. Weavers call their borders *su*, water or stream; hence the main border is *kesme su*, cut or interrupted stream, and the guard border is *ince su*, fine stream, or *seli su*, flowing water. Between the borders is a thin red and white line, a minor guard border called *sekme su*, skipping stream. Lewis refers to it as a "barber's pole stripe" (1920:102). Some weavers call it a *boncuk su,* good luck border.

Many guard borders feature a wavy line resembling a twisted ribbon, known as *sığır sidiği*, trail of bull's urine, or *kadın-kız kaşı*, lady's eyebrow.

All carpets produced by the Yuntdağ cooperative feature the *elibelinde* or arms akimbo border at each kilim end. All carpets from the Ayvacık cooperative have woven tufts in the kilim ends. Some Yuntdağ weavers now add kilim tufts to their designs but these are purely decorative and do not denote village affiliation as they do in the Ayvacık district.

All border motifs in DOBAG carpets have antecendents in the antique carpets on exhibit at the Vakıflar Museum and the Museum of Turkish and Islamic Art in Istanbul. Cammann suggests that continuous borders with "rhythmically recurring elements" are, in Islamic rugs, a metaphor for "the orderly progress of Time, as it proceeds in regular recurring cycles," that is, a cyclical rather than a linear concept of time. This worldview is further enhanced in the borders by the inversion of every second motif, in a sequence of dark and light color, to suggest the contrast between night and day. Cammann also believes that vine and zigzag types of borders, those with inward and outward movements, symbolically carry the idea of dual protection, "shielding those who were seated on the rug within, and at the same time sealing in the good influences that could be helpful to them." The border, therefore, constitutes a "magic barrier." For additional symbolism in border motifs, see Cammann 1972:14-16.

74. Each main border is flanked by two smaller guard borders. A common guard border design is the twisted ribbon known as *sığır sidiği*, trail of bull's urine.

75. Carpets produced by the Yuntdağ cooperative have the arms akimbo or *elibelinde* border at the kilim ends.

76. Carpets produced by the Ayvacık cooperative have a small button tuft in the kilim section.

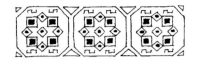

1. *Yıldız,* star, or *yıldız tabak,* stars in boxes.

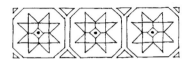

2. Star variant.

3. *Makas,* scissors.

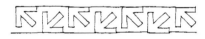

4. *Kazayağı,* goosefeet.

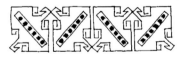

5. *Koca baş,* big head; also known as *koca göt,* big backside, and *kollu,* with arms. This motif is often doubled to give an extrawide border.

6. *Kazan kulpu,* pot or cauldron handle.

7. Simplified *kazan kulpu* design.

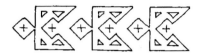

8. *Kazan kulpu* version from a fifteenth-century prayer rug at the Museum of Turkish and Islamic Art.

9. *Urgan,* rope, or *akgül* (literally white rose but used for any floral vine border); also known as *göbek atan,* belly button, in the Yuntdağ region.

10. Vine-type border, also called *üzüm su,* grape border. Cammann sees the endless vine motif as symbolizing continuous time or everlasting life, that is, immortality (1972:14-16).

11. Vine border.

12. *Akgül* type.

13. *Akgül* type.

14. Cennet Deneri calls this border *Koca Mustafa,* Big Mustafa, named after her father. She says the motif originated in the village of Sarıahmetli and her father, Mustafa, brought it to her village, Örselli, for the weavers.

15. *Çiçek,* small blossom, or *karanfil,* carnation.

16. *Çiçek* version, sometimes called *küçük yaprak,* small leaf.

17. *Çiçek* version.

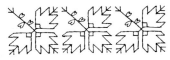

18. *Yaprak su*, leaf border, or *çınar yaprağı*, plane tree leaf.

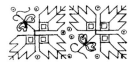

19. Border motif from a nineteenth-century Gördes carpet in the Vakıflar Museum.

20. *Yaprak* border.

21. *Yaprak* version, often doubled in width.

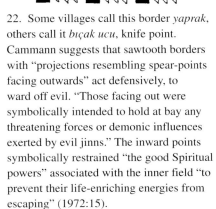

22. Some villages call this border *yaprak*, others call it *bıçak ucu*, knife point. Cammann suggests that sawtooth borders with "projections resembling spear-points facing outwards" act defensively, to ward off evil. "Those facing out were symbolically intended to hold at bay any threatening forces or demonic influences exerted by evil jinns." The inward points symbolically restrained "the good Spiritual powers" associated with the inner field "to prevent their life-enriching energies from escaping" (1972:15).

23. This common border is also known as *yaprak su*, leaf border. Art historians call it the leaf and wine glass border, an appellation that Cammann notes as inappropriate because "Muslims are forbidden to drink alcohol, and when they do so anyway, they use something sturdier than a thin-stemmed goblet; the 'cup' was originally a flower calyx" (1972:14).

24. Leaf and wine glass variant. The Turkish Ministry of Culture catalog refers to the leaf shape as *çakmak*, lighter.

25. Leaf and wine glass variant.

26. Design from a Kazak rug, described as a chalice and oak leaf in the Sotheby Parke Bernet catalog, 14 October 1978, lot no. 13.

27. Border motif described as a serrated leaf and chalice in the Sotheby Parke Bernet catalog, 20 January 1979, lot no. 34.

28. *Lâle*, tulip.

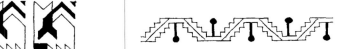

29. *Lâle* version.

59

A

B

C

D

E

F

G

H

30. Derivatives of the S-shape border. Some carpet dealers say the letter S stands for Süleyman the Magnificent. This was, however, a common carpet motif long before Turkey adopted the Roman alphabet in 1928. Whatever its origin, weavers simply call it the S-shape border. Diagram e is known as *aykırı yıldız,* slanting star, or *Örencik su* after the village of that name. Diagram f is also called *baklava su*; baklava is a sweet pastry sliced into rhomboid-shaped pieces.

SCATTER MOTIFS

Small fill-in motifs are scattered throughout the main field of all village carpets. As Gerard Paquin observes, many shapes are stylized representations of familiar objects and the weaver selects images that "express the concerns of everyday life in the village" such as domestic animals, plants, and household utensils (1983:5).

77. Scatter motifs in *çarklı* design.

78. Scatter motifs in *yıldız* design.

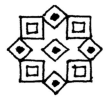

1. *Yıldız*, star.

2. *Deve ayak izi,* camel's footprint.

3. *Göz*, eye.

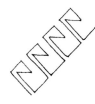

4. *Çengelli,* latchhook, or *kıvrımlı*, curly. Some call it *kaz başi*, goose head.

5. *Ibrik,* water ewer. The ewer is associated with ritual cleansing before entering the mosque for prayer, and is also a basic household water container. Cammann sees the ewer as symbolic of "life-giving water" (1972:20).

6. *Muska* or *hamayıl, a* suspended "magic triangle" or good luck symbol. In parts of the Middle East, jewelry in the form of a triangular pendant functions as an amulet to protect the wearer against the evil eye. The shape is often doubled in Turkish carpet designs.

7. *Tarak,* comb. Comblike forms are common in Islamic rugs and Paquin suggests that they are good luck charms rather than hair combs (1983:16). Some weavers call it *kırkıt* after the comb-shaped beater used to compact the weft while weaving. Cammann dismisses these explanations: "It seems more likely that this was once a very ancient symbol of rain descending from the sky, which originally connoted life-giving waters, just as the vase or ewer did" (1972:20).

8. *Basit elma*, simple apple.

9. *Elibelinde*, arm's akimbo.

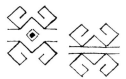

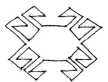

10. Similar to the *elibelinde* motif is the *koç boynuzu,* ram's horn, or *koç başi,* ram's head.

11. *Yar küstü,* lovers' quarrel.

12. *Akrep,* scorpion.

13. *Kavak yaprak,* poplar leaf.

14. *Gül,* rosette.

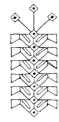 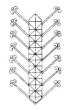

15. *Hayat ağacı,* tree of life.

VILLAGE LIFE

By the 1980s, carpet making as a cottage industry had reached a low ebb in the villages of western Turkey. The reintroduction of natural dyes revitalized both the carpets and the market. Carpets were converted to cash and the standard of living improved for cooperative members.

The DOBAG project also brought weavers and their families into greater contact with the outside world; foreign buyers are frequent visitors to the villages, and Marmara University staff are a regular presence. Weavers travel abroad, as far afield as Japan and the United States, to give educational demonstrations of carpet making. Thus, village people are exposed to new ideas and urban attitudes. To what extent have these influences, combined with a steady flow of cash, altered the traditional way of life? Has the establishment of the two cooperatives had a positive or negative impact on village communities over the past fifteen years?

In western Turkey, village society remains conservative, the pace of life is slow, and people do not readily accept change. New is not necessarily better, as it is in many Western countries where fads come and go and we relish innovation. The most important thing in the life of every villager is the family — the backbone of the community. Conformity is valued, and children grow up with modest goals — to marry, have children, be able to support the family, and to stay in the village where they belong. Thus, there is close, daily contact between the generations.

Modern birth-control methods have been available in local pharmacies since the 1960s, gradually becoming commonplace even in remote areas such as the Yuntdağ. Hence, family size is small, averaging four family members (Powell 1987); the 1980 national census shows an average of 5.2 in rural areas. In one village, Süleymanköy, in 1990 there were 280 inhabitants but only eight school children.

The importance of family bonds was made clear to me when the California Academy of Sciences first invited village weavers to the museum in 1990. I had assumed that women who had never left their villages would be clamoring for adventure and excited at the opportunity to visit the United States. I expected some rivalry in choosing two representative weavers. This was not the case. Women are reluctant to leave their families for two to three weeks. The main advantage to them is that they can buy American consumer goods to take back as gifts for their children and husbands, and there is a certain amount of social status is being the only person in the village to have traveled by airplane to a foreign country.

Villagers are of the Sünni sect of Islam, and the women are not to be confused with the usual stereotype of Muslim fundamentalist women, secluded and completely covered from head to toe. They do cover their hair and arms in public, but Turkish village women no longer veil their faces. This practice was outlawed in Turkey in 1926, along with a ban on the traditional fez worn by men. When Mustafa Kemal Atatürk became the first president of the new republic in 1923, he transferred the seat of government from Istanbul to Ankara and embarked on a policy of Westernization and secularization, with a civil code replacing the law of the Koran. Turkey adopted the Gregorian calendar in 1926, and the Roman alphabet replaced Arabic script in 1928.

Though Islam is the predominant religion, non-Muslims are free to worship as they wish. Turkish Muslims do not strictly follow the dietary taboos and moral codes usually adhered to in Islamic Arab countries, especially those concerning women. Turkish women are not forbidden from entering a mosque; there is a special prayer section where they can worship. Moreover, while the countryside remains socially and sexually conservative, Turkish women in large cities are as sophisticated as any in Europe. These high-powered, professional women in the fields of law, medicine, engineering, and higher education challenge Islamic conformity. Turkey had a woman prime minister, Tansu Çiller, from 1993 to 1996.

79. Village women socializing. Süleymanköy 1995.

Village women work hard and keep busy at all times. Even when socializing in groups outside their houses, women spin, weave, embroider, darn socks, knit, or crotchet while keeping an eye on the children. One of many daily tasks, weaving must be integrated into the household routine. In the summer, women and children help the men in the fields; therefore weavers usually have more time for weaving between September and May, when the crops are harvested.

In contrast, men have more time on their hands; their work in the fields is seasonal and erratic, and only a few have animals to herd. Enter any village and the first sight is of men sitting around in groups near or inside the tea house (*kahve*), socializing. The tea house is not the domain of women. When the DOBAG team from Marmara University first visited Süleymanköy, they wanted to meet the weavers as a group and therefore held a general meeting in the *kahve*. It was the first time women had ever set foot in the village teahouse (Powell 1987).

Before the cooperatives existed, family incomes were low. Men's earning capacity was, and still is, limited, and women sold their inferior carpets to dealers for a mere pittance. The DOBAG project's impact was twofold: It restored the quality of the carpets, enabling the villages to produce a commercially viable item, and it provided a guaranteed export market with above-average prices for the weaver's work, improving economic conditions for the entire family. Between 1982 and 1988, the income of families in the cooperative increased well above the national average for rural areas.

Weavers receive substantial sums for their carpets on a regular basis, thus the woman's share of the family income has increased dramatically. In a few cases, the weaver's export bonus alone surpasses her husband's total annual income, making the woman the main provider. This represents a major shift in gender roles within the family's economic support system.

However, the increased income generated by female members of the family has not altered the expenditure pattern within the family. The one who earns the money is not necessarily the one who spends it. Men customarily handle the household expenses, and most women hand over their carpet money to their husbands. The status quo remains intact, as does the male ego. However, husband and wife jointly make decisions on how the money is used and, although they do not have outright control of spending, women now have more influence on buying decisions than they had previously. Thus, the power structure within the village family has not been disrupted, as yet. But change is in the air.

In the Ayvacık cooperative, where the men make up the membership, some women think that they, not their husbands, should receive the money directly. On one occasion I met a disgruntled weaver working at her loom, who commented: "If he gets the money, let him weave the carpets!" It was significant that she didn't attempt to hide her feelings of resentment, even to an outsider, and didn't hesitate to voice her opinions openly, reinforcing my initial impression of these village women as strong, feisty individuals who are not afraid to express their minds and who do not always kowtow to the men. Another woman whose husband collected the money on her behalf was asked if she would spend the money differently. "I would probably buy the same things but I might get them cheaper!" (Powell 1987).

These are not isolated instances of overt defiance. Whereas most village women accept their position in the family hierarchy and are not about to usurp the husband's status as head of the household, the situation could change in the near future. Şerife Ergün, a weaver from Süleymanköy village, recently admitted that she does not hand over her money to her husband, and that other women are doing the same. The battle of the sexes is about to begin!

80. Typical outdoor stone oven.
    Süleymanköy 1992.

81. Television aerial. Sarıahmetli, 1995.

With new wealth, how are cooperative members using the money? Has affluence, by village standards, affected their lifestyle? Villagers still wear the same clothing and eat the same food, though now they can afford more meat in their diet. They still buy the same daily essentials, but possibly in greater quantities than before. A few villagers have increased their livestock and purchased land. Others paid off debts or were able to afford circumcision ceremonies and lavish weddings (Powell 1987). Several communities installed a piped water supply and a sewage system. All the villages now have electricty, and many families bought durable goods such as radios, televisions (usually the first major purchase), refrigerators, space heaters, and butane gas stoves for cooking and boiling tea. However, women continue to bake bread in large, stone, outdoor ovens fueled by firewood. Economic betterment has improved living conditions but does not appear to have radically changed local folklife.

The electrical appliances are not necessarily used. A television set, proudly displayed in a corner of the room, might be a sign of prestige rather than a source of nightly entertainment. When Cennet Deneri visited San Francisco in 1991, she bought a wristwatch for her husband. The following year, when I took tea in her house in Örselli, I noticed the watch, still in its original box, in a prominent position on top of the television. By 1995 Cennet's television corner, now almost shrinelike, included the same watch, a cellular telephone still in its package, a battery clock, and an electric wall clock, alongside an assortment of vases, a mirror, five calendars, framed certificates, and family photographs.

A further change in Cennet's house, over a four-year period, was the appearance of furniture. On my first visit we sat on cushions on the floor and ate in the traditional manner, from a large circular tray resting on a wooden frame. Cennet, who is currently the president of the Yuntdağ cooperative, has now bought a sofabed, two couches, a kitchen table, and chairs. Cennet's house is not unusual. Other families have followed suit and bought Western-style furniture. In most cases these houses belong to weavers who have traveled internationally to promote carpets and

82. Cennet Deneri's television corner. Örselli 1995.

83. Dudu Öztoprak at home. Süleymanköy 1996.

have visited Western homes. Generally, though, most house interiors remain traditional with one exception — the television set (there are now twelve Turkish television channels). The houses I visited typically had one large room dominated by the loom. There were carpets and cushions on the floor and a television set in the corner, but nothing else. Hanging bags and shelves provide storage, and bedding is unrolled at night and spread on the floor.

DOBAG carpets made from natural dyes fetch high prices. To villagers, they are first and foremost a commodity and their high value prohibits their use as floor coverings in their own homes. They keep for themselves only those carpets that fall short of the strict quality requirements of the cooperatives. Money from the sale of a single DOBAG carpet can purchase quantities of machine-made rugs for the wear and tear of daily use. An eclectic assortment of small overlapping rugs (a similar arrangement to the carpets in any mosque) completely covers the floor space in the typical village home — machine-made Belgian rugs, old and threadbare handmade carpets in village designs (usually with aniline dyes) and, predominantly, colorful flatweaves.

Families with unmarried sons are apt to invest their money in gold jewelry for the bride's dowry. Although there is no longer a bride price, customarily the groom's family presents the future bride with an agreed-upon gift of gold coins and jewelry upon the couple's engagement. The coins can be worn on a necklace or sewn to the edge of a headscarf for public

84. Village house. Örselli 1995.

85. Machine-made carpets for sale at the Friday market. Ayvacık 1995.

67

display. There are two types of coins — the *reşat,* minted in the nineteenth century, and a twentieth-century equivalent called *cumhuriyet.* Newspapers publish the currency value of the coins daily, and they can be converted to cash at the stated price in any market town. Although the gold belongs to the girl, as her personal property, the community expects the couple to use it for major expenses, or as a hedge against inflation, or even in case of unexpected financial hardship. However, the young woman exercises some control; she must be consulted and agree to its spending (Powell 1987).

87. A young weaver with her dowry chest and dowry carpets. Çamkalabak 1992. (Photo Harald Böhmer)

Parents want their children to have a good start in life, and providing a decent dowry is important to them. Usually a family has to sell land or other valuables to buy the jewelry. The groom's father also donates a house and some of the furnishings. The bride's family contributes rugs and other textiles, many woven by the girl herself.

Although parents still arrange, or rather facilitate, marriages, they do not force a girl to marry against her will. In Çamkalabak, a village of recently settled Yörüks, wedding festivities last for days, during which time the guests visit the bride's home to inspect the entire dowry, especially the large quantity of carpets and flatweaves on display. As a form of stored wealth, some textiles are kept in reserve for hard times, and may never be used in the couple's new home. A caravan of three or four camels, hired for the occasion, escorts the bride to her future home on her wedding day. Laden with the dowry textiles, called *çeyiz,* the procession offers a further opportunity for public display of the girl's weaving skills and her family's wealth (Atlıhan 1993:86-87).

86. Fatma Ergun's *çeyiz.* Süleymanköy 1995.

For sleeping and living, the traditional stone house has one multipurpose room with a fireplace. Interiors are dark. There are either no windows at all or one small window, and the weavers rely on light from the open door when working inside. However, the huge looms take up a large amount of space, and many weavers work outdoors, weather permitting. Women who work for the cooperative want to weave all year round, and a few families have used their money to add an extra room onto the house, specifically to accommodate the loom and store weaving materials. These large rooms, enhanced with overhead fluorescent strip lighting, offer a permanent indoor work area that is comfortable during the cold winter. Some houses have expanded upward, with an added story. In certain villages, therefore, as a direct result of the cooperatives, the vernacular architecture has been adapted to meet the weavers' needs.

The addition of an entire room onto a house primarily for "women's work" indicates the importance of the weaver within the family and her respected position within the community. The add-on room, as an investment in future finances, reflects the new status of village weavers as principal providers. The change in architecture correlates with the change in the women's social standing.

Carpet making is profitable and, for some women, weaving takes priority in the work schedule. Because women can earn more money weaving carpets for sale than they can working in the fields, they often pay someone else to take their turn during the summer months. Further evidence that weaving is indeed serious business is the willingness of husbands to take on the domestic duties of their wives. Men as well as women are facing change; they now help with milking, collecting firewood, and other household tasks, giving the women more time at the loom. That the men cooperate and accept the switch in gender roles, in a traditionally male-dominated society, signifies the power of financial incentive over social custom.

Accelerated carpet production has revitalized subsiduary crafts for the men too. They help gather plants and dye the wool, they carve the spindles and whorls, build looms, construct spinning wheels, fashion wooden combs and beaters, hammer copper sheep bells, and help in the carpet depot as van drivers, delivery men, guards, and bookkeepers.

Village society frowns upon divorce. A widowed woman receives family support; a divorced woman is considered an outcast, and few women would choose to bring up their children alone, alienated from their families. Bill McDonnell tells the story of a weaver he met during a visit to Turkey in 1995, a divorced woman whose life improved entirely because she was a member of the cooperative. Withholding her real name, he calls her Hatice (1995:3). The victim of spousal abuse for many years, Hatice was in her early thirties, the mother of three children. Rather than continue the way she lived, she chose to become a "second-class citizen" and get a divorce. A member of the cooperative, Hatice was a talented weaver and was elected to represent the cooperative at weaving demonstrations in other countries. She regained her self-confidence and was able to provide for her children without financial assistance.

"She often returned from trips speaking a little of that country's language and bringing new ideas to her village. It wasn't long before she attained a position of prestige and importance in the village. The cooperative provided her with a vehicle to reestablish herself as an independent woman and claim her position as a valued member of her village." Hatice's story has a happy ending: She met the love of her life and remarried — a rare occurrence, for normally a divorced woman with children never remarries.

In the Yuntdağ cooperative, operated by the weavers, a few women have learned new skills in managing finances, developing marketing strategies,

88. Bell-maker. Ayvacık fair 1992.

89. Mustafa Sezgin carves wooden beaters. Süleymanköy 1995.

and in public relations — positions of leadership within the community normally held by men. Not all women may want to enter the sphere of business, but at least the cooperative has given them the opportunity, and some have become successful in this milieu and gained self-confidence in decision making and their new work status outside the home.

By branching out into the business world, the Yuntdağ women provide new role models for their daughters. Cooperative weavers are also economically successful mothers — a further positive role model for village girls. And, with potential earning power, daughters are more of a resource to the family than are sons, and the imperative need for a male heir pales as a result. Mothers consider it an advantage to have a daughter to assist them with carpet weaving, which generates income. This appreciation influences a girl's self-image and reinforces feelings of self-worth. Moreover, the young women's interest in learning carpet weaving should ensure that the tradition carries on into the next generation.

A woman's weaving ability is one of her main assets as a wife and, along with good health and other traits fitting for village life, is one of the desirable qualities a young man looks for in a prospective partner rather than beauty and appearance. Nowadays, girls with exceptional weaving skills are much in demand, for weavers in the cooperatives can make good money — a situation that further enhances a young women's self-esteem. When the Ayvacık cooperative started, four hopeful bachelors, with a view to improved economic conditions, took out membership to secure places for their future wives (Powell 1987). With the prospect of earning more than their husbands, and the promise of a secure and regular income, dextrous young weavers have become exceedingly eligible, which in turn gives them bargaining power and a certain amount of control in choosing a mate. Although match-making parents maneuver young people together, a girl with many suitors has more options. In these cases, the responsibility of choosing a mate has shifted from male to female.

All village girls learn to weave at around seven or eight years of age. In the past, poor families desperately in need of cash sent their young daughters to work outside the home in weaving workshops where they were apprenticed for long hours and very little pay. Prospective buyers of DOBAG carpets in the United States often ask if the cooperatives use child labor. In light of periodic reports in the media of exploitation in the textile industries in the Middle East and India, and of horror stories of the past, this is a legitimate concern. According to one report from 1920, in Sivas "there are factories in which are employed many thousand little girls, ages ranging from four years upward. They work from twelve to fourteen hours a day and the largest amount received

by them is five piastres (less than twenty cents). These factories are hotbeds of tuberculosis. This amount of money scarcely keeps them in bread and in this underfed condition, working so long in ill-ventilated rooms, they quickly succumb to this disease" (Lewis 1920:33).

In Turkey today, eight years of education is compulsory, so child labor in most rural areas has been effectively eliminated. Yet, as recently as the 1970s, factories were still employing children as carpet knotters. Barbara Bigelow visited such a set-up, the Sümerbank Hereke Fabrikası, founded in Hereke in the mid-nineteenth century, where she saw girls of all ages sitting on rows of wooden benches at their looms, copying from designs on graph paper. "I was so shocked at the ages of some of the girls who sat knotting from dawn till dusk for so little in the way of salary. It appears that the very young girls are preferred because they are the most eager and ambitious, most easily trained, and are without any marriage or family ties to demand their time" (1972:13). Fortunately, this situation is now a thing of the past. In 1994 I visited two carpet factories in Turkey, in Bergama and Cappadocia, that employed unmarried girls; they appeared to be between sixteen and nineteen years of age, well past school age.

In the villages, there is a plentiful supply of young weavers who are learning from their mothers at the loom, but the cooperatives do not accept carpets from girls under eighteen years of age. Furthermore, the high prices paid to the weavers discourage the temptation to supplement incomes from child labor.

Families with cooperative membership earn more money than other families do, causing discrepancies in personal material wealth among villagers that can at times lead to resentment and envy. Some houses have television aerials; others do not. However, frequently the money is used for the common good, such as improving water supplies and sewage systems or renovating or rebuilding the local mosque, and the village as a whole benefits.

Village weavers who do not work for the cooperatives have also benefited indirectly from the rediscovered knowledge of plant dyes. Dr. Böhmer's dye recipes were copied and soon spread from village to village when weavers realized that naturally dyed carpets could fetch high prices on the open market —

three to four times more for *kök boya* than *anilin boya*. The elevated prices paid by the cooperatives gave all local weavers bargaining power with dealers. Knowing full well the value of their carpets, women learned to hold out for their asking price. Thus the cooperatives have helped all village weavers to get fair compensation for their work. As one Çamkalabak woman remarked: "If the cooperative stopped existing, things would quickly go back to what they had been in 1981 when the dealers could bring the price down and play the weavers one against the other" (Powell 1987).

The numerous small shops in the town of Ayvacık that are now competitively selling naturally dyed carpets, as well as those with mixed dyes, attest to the cooperative's impact on the region. In the neighboring village of Assos, a colorful array of carpets, draped over stone walls or hanging from trees, greets the tourist buses. The carpets look like DOBAG rugs — traditional village designs in muted, natural colors — though they are not subject to the cooperative's strict quality controls. During my visit to Assos in 1991, an elderly village man, cashing in on DOBAG's reputation, ran after me shouting his sales pitch. "Look, all natural dyes, just like the German professor," referring to Dr. Harald Böhmer.

The return to natural dyes in village carpet making boosted the local economy, and slowed down migration to the cities. A few families actually moved back to the area. One of the reasons for the cooperatives' success, at the village level, rests with the decision not to organize weavers into management-controlled workshops to weave under contract — a system prevalent in other parts of Turkey — or to impose alien designs from outside the culture. Removing women from their homes and families would be contrary to DOBAG's mission — to revitalize carpet weaving without endangering the social foundation of the community.

Women continue to follow the established custom of weaving at home, surrounded by friends and relatives. In this comfortable milieu, where weaving fits into the round of daily chores, the weaver works when and where she chooses, and at her own speed. She picks her own colors, materials, and size for her rugs. Rather than rigidly following a graph-paper cartoon, or pattern, the weaver can be flexible,

improvising and freely interpreting traditional patterns. The finished carpet is hers, to sell to whom she pleases, though weavers rarely sell their work on the free market, which pays less than the cooperative does. This self-employed status fosters independence and personal satisfaction, and conforms to standard village folkways.

The renaissance of natural dyes has had a ripple effect outside the immediate vicinity. Harald Böhmer's easy-to-follow dye recipes proved so successful that, before long, photocopies spread throughout Turkey. Once, during a trip to a remote weaving area, Dr. Böhmer was surprised to find dyers using his methods. They explained that they learned indigo dyeing from "instructions from a professor at the university" who had never actually visited their village. They proceeded to show Böhmer a copy of one of his own leaflets, complete with his name and that of Marmara University (Thompson 1986:16).

During the 1980s naturally dyed carpets began appearing in Istanbul and other urban centers. According to Josephine Powell, "there is no doubt that the idea of natural dyed rugs has caught on. There is not a dealer in Istanbul or Izmir who does not stock them. They may be pale, clipped refugees from the acid baths of the bazaar wash-houses, but they are prominently displayed and proudly discussed. People who, after an absence of several years, come to Istanbul all notice that the whole color scheme of the rug bazaar has changed, infinitely for the better. The DOBAG project has set in motion a return to the old color relationships and pride in Anatolian village designs" (1987).

To sum up, the DOBAG project has been instrumental in conserving a folk-art tradition. It restored the integrity of the village carpet by reclaiming the lost knowledge of natural dyeing without attempting to modify or influence village carpet designs, color schemes, or local customs associated with weaving as a domestic activity. Women continue to control the aesthetics and to work at home as they always have done. The project built on an existing textile tradition rather than impose new ideas external to the culture. As such, DOBAG reforged a link with the past, and villagers regained a part of their artistic heritage.

Additionally, the cooperative provided a guaranteed market for the carpets, at high prices, to ensure a reliable income for weavers. The influx of cash improved living conditions for weavers and their families. Some, but not all, villagers bought modern electrical appliances and acquired other material possessions — embellishments to daily life — and some enlarged their houses. However, changes in the situation of cooperative members do not apply to the entire village population. The long-term effects on the community remain to be seen.

The most telling change in the traditional way of life is that numerous village women are now the main providers, contributing more money than their husbands do to the family income. Their economic success, as both carpet weavers and, in some instances, as businesswomen, has elevated the social standing of women within the community. Nevertheless, although some of the men are willing to help with household chores, the hierarchy and power structure within the family still follow convention. The project has not drastically interfered with the sociocultural underpinnings of village life; the collective ideology and worldview, the shared values, beliefs, and mores remain the same.

The DOBAG project has proved that economics can be a strong force in the conservation of a marginal folk art, and that people barely subsisting will be motivated to maintain crafts that generate income. A flourishing market provides an incentive to produce quality work and continue the tradition. And the carpet-making tradition includes commodification, for in this region carpets have always been traded.

The buyers also play a role in nurturing folk art. The steady demand internationally for DOBAG carpets sends a message to villagers that the outside world acknowledges their skills and accomplishments. Appreciation of the art object and, by extension, its maker, boosts morale and further encourages and reinforces a group's commitment to conserving their art. Outside interest and enthusiasm validate the folk expression. When others care about a group's traditions, the group will too; when others place value on the handmade object, so will the makers. When individuals are motivated to maintain their traditional art, driven by a sense of pride in who they are and their own cultural heritage, its future is assured.

Village weavers travel regularly to foreign countries such as the United States to promote their carpets through public demonstrations. When they receive admiration and respect for their work, and a positive response to themselves as Turkish women, they take that back with them to the village. Over the years, the weavers have interacted with many people — in museums, carpet galleries, schools, cultural centers — who, unknowingly, have contributed in a small way to the perpetuation of the Turkish village carpet.

During my last visit to Turkey in 1997, I revisited village mosques to look again at pre-DOBAG carpets, those made in the death throes of a textile tradition. Compared to a 1990s village carpet, glowing with color, the earlier versions are noticeably inferior in technique and general quality, many lying alongside factory copies bought at local markets. However, although the DOBAG project brought handknotted village carpets back from the grave, their survival now rests with the women who make them.

Each carpet expresses the weaver's identity and her place in the world. It embodies individual creativity, family designs, regional variations, and a Turkish aesthetic. It also represents her history, a cultural legacy handed down from generations of weavers before her. As part of this continuum, the weaver's designs and skills will pass to her daughter, to be carried into the future where village carpet making will, it is hoped, remain a living folk art as strong as it is today, and there will be no need of a second coming. Cooperatives such as DOBAG may come and go, but it is only the weavers themselves who can breathe new life into an old tradition and ensure its continuation.

90. The next generation of weavers. Çamkalabak 1992.

92. Sarıahmetli 1995.

73

91. Bahriye Ercan and her daughter, Nurdane. Çamkalabak 1992.

BIBLIOGRAPHY

Acar, Belkıs Balpınar. *Kilim, Cicim, Zili, Sumak.*
Istanbul: Eren Yayinlari, 1982.

—. *Carpets of the Vakıflar Museum Istanbul.*
Wesel: Uta Hülsey, 1988.

Atlıhan, Şerife. "Traditional Weavings in One Village
of Settled Nomads in Northwest Anatolia."
Oriental Carpet and Textile Studies, 4, 1993.

Ayyıldız, Uğur. *Contemporary Handmade Turkish
Carpets.* Istanbul: NET Turizm Ticaret ve Sanayi,
1982.

Bigelow, Barbara. "Visit to a Turkish Carpet Factory."
Craft Horizons, June 1972.

Blum, Walter. "The Man Who Gave Away His Rugs."
California Living Magazine, 8 March 1981.

Böhmer, Harald. "The Revival of Natural Dyeing in
Two Weaving Areas of Anatolia."
Oriental Rug Review, 3, no. 9, 1983.

—. "Carpets from the Yuntdağ Region in Western
Anatolia." *Oriental Carpet and Textile Studies*, 3,
no. 2, 1989.

Böhmer, Harald, and Werner Brüggemann. *Rugs of
the Peasants and Nomads of Anatolia.*
München: Kunst und Antiquitaten, 1983.

Böhmer, Harald, and Jon Thompson. "The Pazyryk
Carpet: A Technical Discussion." *Source: Notes in the
History of Art,* 10, no. 4, 1991.

Cammann, Schuyler V. R. "Symbolic Meanings in
Oriental Rug Patterns." *Textile Museum Journal*, 3,
no. 3, 1972.

Carroll, Diane Lee. *Looms and Textiles of the Copts.*
San Francisco: California Academy of Sciences,
1988.

Cootner, Cathryn. *Tent and Town.*
San Francisco: Fine Arts Museums of San Francisco,
1982.

Davies, Peter. *The Tribal Eye: Antique Kilims of
Anatolia.* New York: Rizzoli International, 1993.

Denny, Walter B. "Anatolian Rugs: An Essay on
Method." *Textile Museum Journal,* 3, no. 4, 1973.

Durul, Yusuf. *Yörük Kılımlerí Nığde Yöresı.*
Istanbul: Ak Yayinlari, 1977.

Eiland, Murray L., Jr. *Oriental Rugs from Pacific
Collections.* San Francisco: San Francisco Bay Area
Rug Society, 1990.

Eiland, Murray L., III. "DOBAG II: A Second Look
at the DOBAG Project." *Oriental Rug Review,* 15, no.
3, 1995.

Erdmann, Kurt. *The History of the Early Turkish
Carpet.* London: Oguz, 1977.

Eren, A. Nacı. *Turkish Handmade Carpets.*
Istanbul: Hıtıt Color, 1992.

Ferrero, Mercedes Viale. *Rare Carpets.*
London: Orbis Books, 1972.

Ford, P. R. J. *The Oriental Carpet.*
New York: Harry N. Abrams, 1981.

Garret, Gayle. "DOBAG at Seven." *Oriental Rug
Review,* 8, no. 4, 1988.

Glassie, Henry. *Turkish Traditional Art Today.*
Bloomington, Indiana: Indiana University Press,
1993.

Hecht, Ann. *The Art of the Loom.*
New York: Rizzoli International, 1989.

Hubel, Reinhard G. *The Book of Carpets.*
New York: Praeger, 1970.

Hunter, George Leland. "The Truth About Doctored
Rugs." *Country Life in America,* July 1906: 333-36.

Landreau, Anthony N., Anita Landreau, and
Ralph S. Yohe. *Flowers of the Yayla: Yoruk Weaving
of the Toros Mountains.* Washington, D.C.: Textile
Museum, 1983.

Lewis, George Griffin. *The Practical Book of
Oriental Carpets.* Philadelphia: Lippincott, 1920.

McDonnell, Bill. "A Happy Ending." *Return to Tradition* newsletter, 1, no. 2, 1995.

Mackie, Louise W. *The Splendor of Turkish Weaving.* Washington, D.C.: Textile Museum, 1973.

McMullan, Joseph V., ed. *Turkish Rugs: The Rachel B. Stevens Memorial Collection.* Washington, D.C.: Textile Museum, 1972.

Opie, James. *Tribal Rugs of Southern Persia.* Portland: James Opie Oriental Rugs, Inc., 1981.

—. "Approaching Rug Motifs as a Language." *Oriental Carpet and Textile Studies,* 4, 1993.

Paquin, Gerard A. "The Iconography of Everyday Life in Nineteenth-Century Middle Eastern Rugs." *Textile Museum Journal,* 22, 1983.

Pekın, Ersu. *Turkish Flatweaves and Carpets.* Istanbul: Mınyatür Yayınları, 1988.

Peterson, Jane. "A Passion for Color." *Aramco World,* 42, no. 3, 1991.

Pinner, Robert. "The Crivelli Rug Medallion and the Turkmen Connection." *Oriental Carpet and Textile Studies,* 4, 1993.

Powell, Josephine. "Ala Cuval." *Oriental Rug Review,* 5, no. 2, 1985.

—. *The DOBAG Weavers in the Villages around Ayvacık: Tradition and Change.* Paper presented at the International Conference on Oriental Carpets, Georgetown University, Virginia, 10 May 1987.

Quataert, Donald. "The Carpet-Makers of Western Anatolia, 1750-1914." *Textile Museum Journal,* 25, 1986.

Raby, J. "Court and Export: Market Demands in Ottoman Carpets 1450-1550." *Oriental Carpet and Textile Studies,* 2, 1986.

Robinson, Stuart. *A History of Dyed Textiles.* London: Studio Vista, 1969.

Sakhai, Essie. *The Story of Carpets.* London: Studio Editions, 1991.

Saltzman, Max. "Identifying Dyes in Textiles." *American Scientist,* 80, 1992:474-81.

Schlosser, Ignace. *The Book of Rugs.* New York: Bonanza Books, 1963.

Sommer, John Lambert, and Lois Sommer Kreider. *Anatolian Carpets: A Family Connection.* North Newton, Kansas: Kauffman Museum, 1986.

Thompson, Jon. "Centralised Designs." In Eberhart Herrmann, *Von Konya bis Kokand,* München, 1982:7-27.

—. "A Return to Tradition." *Hali,* April 1986.

Thompson, Jon, and Louise W. Mackie. *Turkmen Tribal Carpets and Traditions.* Washington D.C.: Textile Museum, 1980.

Wertime, John T. "Flatwoven Structures Found in Nomadic and Village Weavings from the Near East and Central Asia." *Textile Museum Journal,* 18, 1979.

Winitz, Jan David. "The Language of Symbolism in Tribal Oriental Rugs." *Report.* San Francisco Crafts and Folk Art Museum, 1985.

Yetkin, Şerare. *Early Caucasian Carpets in Turkey,* 2 vols. London: Oguz, 1978.

—. *Historical Turkish Carpets.* Istanbul: Türkıye iş Bankasi Cultural Publications, 1981.

93. Turkish weavers visiting the United States are fascinated with their first look at a Guatemalan backstrap loom. Santa Perfitt, from the Mam Indian village of Todos Santos de Cuchamatan, demonstrates her weaving skills at the California Academy of Sciences, 1994. (Photo David Jacobson)

INDEX